suncatchers in my windows

suncatchers in my windows

A Collection of Personal Essays

Odessa S. Snyder

Mountain State Press
Charleston, West Virginia

Five essays, Lest We Forget, High Energy Level — Asset or Liability?, Handicaps Can Have Compensations, The New Dimension, and The Heritage, are new to this publication. All others were published (many were under different titles, some have been revised) in the weekday morning or Sunday editions of The Journal, Martinsburg, West Virginia, between March 20, 1991 and July 2, 1992.

International Standard Book Number: 0-941092-25-9

Library of Congress Catalog Card number: 92-61483

Mountain State Press
c/o The University of Charleston
2300 MacCorkle Avenue, S.E.
Charleston, WV 25304

Printed in the United States of America

Photographs by: Odessa S. Snyder and her granddaughter Natalie Snyder

This is a Mountain State Press book produced in affiliation with the University of Charleston, Charleston, West Virginia. Mountain State Press is solely responsible for editorial decisions.

FOR

My children and their partners:

Nick and Mimi

Beth and Thomas

Table of Contents

No Price Tag On Suncatchers

On a sunny morning, my upstairs hall can be enchanting. A round, crystal suncatcher in the window shoots out rainbows that spatter around the room-size hall, up the attic stairs and down to the landing below. Touch it lightly (not too hard, or the glass pane will crack!) and dozens of miniature rainbows will dart about like an iridescent will-o'-the-wisp. So often, I sit in the century-old, oak rocking chair and just watch. I'm not upset when one cluster of rainbows disappears because I know that in a moment, dozens more will be flitting about.

A special niece of mine in Kentucky gave me the suncatcher, and I've so much wanted to purchase a similar one for the southeast window over my desk in the dining room. I've peered into many shop windows and walked on by because the price tag discouraged me

And then I rationalized — do I really need suncatchers that hang in windows? Not long ago my daughter's family and I were on our way to a concert in Montgomery, Alabama. Just at twilight, on the left side of a quiet street, we came to a tall, white church, elegant in its architectural simplicity. On top, within the dome, was a huge, stained-glass window, half-circle in shape, absolutely magnificent in color and design. Through its panes came the evening sun, highlighting the gorgeous hues of the window and pushing streams of color like an arched bridge into the street below.

Strange, the sight was so beautiful, so awesome that no one spoke, total silence in the car.

Suddenly, the six-year-old, with her enormous, dreamy, brown eyes fastened on the window whispered, "God, that's darlin'!" Her unusual exclamation was neither blasphemous nor inappropriate. There is no softer word in our language than "darling," and if we call God's name when we are touched by something of beauty, it's a way of giving Him credit!

Recently, a close friend came for supper, bringing me a majestic, porcelain eagle perched on a tree-stump pedestal. He does not glitter nor cast rainbows nor pick up the pink and purple rays of the morning light, but he stands poised with wings outspread, ready to fly into the sun, or possibly to soar above the storm clouds.

The money plant (some call it the "penny" plant) doesn't cast rainbows either, but when the sun touches its silky leaves, any corner can be radiant. On an old table near me, the money plant leaves with their soft, velvety sheen form a halo for sprays of crimson princess feather in a miniature washbowl and pitcher set. The arrangement brings in, not only the sunshine but pleasant memories of Jim, my husband, whose love for growing things brightens my day even after he has gone.

Right now, the midday sun has pushed back the shadows on the quaint smokehouse outside my window. Storms have faded the shingles, and the padlock on the door is rusty because no one cures hams anymore, but the big bell in the tower still sounds. When a grandchild sneaks up and grasps the heavy wire attached to the clapper, a clear, vibrant peal tolls out memories of a long procession of field workers hurrying in for noontime "dinner." No longer does the bell summon workers to dinner; we just ring it for fun! Some bells have a sad sound. This one doesn't. It rings out a happy knell in cheerful, tenor tones!

To me, anything of beauty, anything that speaks of love and caring, any memory that makes me feel warm and safe inside is a suncatcher.

I'II always enjoy my crystal ball in the upstairs hall. I'll continue to sit in the rocker and watch the rainbows play up and down the stairway, but I'll stop shopping for other suncatchers. Even on cloudy days, it seems I've so many suncatchers in my world. They glow long after the sun sinks behind the apple orchard even after darkness closes in and there are no price tags attached!

Everybody needs a window that catches the morning sun.

Don't Take My Wheels!

When I broke my leg, long before the doctor finished putting on the cast, I asked, "How long will it be before I can drive?"

When I had eye surgery, knowing I never did see out of one eye and the other eye was still covered with a patch, I asked, "How long will it be before I can drive?"

If my car doesn't go out the lane all day, my neighbors who live below me, often call and ask, "Dess, are you all right?"

If my son notices the car has remained stationary over a twelve hour period, he will drop in from the dairy by nightfall and query, "What's wrong with you?"

Maybe I enjoy my wheels because for over half of my life I was without them. I was nearing forty when I learned to drive, and I'll admit it was the most difficult, most nerve-wracking mechanical accomplishment of my life before or since.

Things have changed, though. I am now an arrogant driver — not arrogant in that I think I'm an expert driver; I doubt that I even rank borderline average. I'm arrogant in that when I drive, I see no one. My friends wave at me and I never know it; acquaintances blow horns and I never hear them; I see no corn fields ripening in the July sun nor fence rows laden with snow in the winter time. I see only the road ahead of me. Perhaps my readers on the Summit Point road will feel safer now, and my friends will forgive me for ignoring them.

Along with accepting my limitations and attempting to adjust accordingly, I look back over the last thirty years and feel that still another factor has entered into my colorful driving career. Actually, this may sound to you like something out of science fiction or akin to a voyage into the land of psychic powers. My cars have been abnormally — almost supernaturally — kind to me!

The only one that constantly refused to do my bidding was, coincidentally or not, the only new one I ever owned. It stopped every time I slowed down for a curve; I tried not slowing down, but it stopped anyway. Could it be that all the used cars had been broken in by others as inept as I, thereby adapting their motors and transmissions to the eccentricities and weaknesses of former owners? Somehow, so far, my cars have sheltered me, protected me, and covered for my inadequacies.

On a bitter cold, snowy, January morning the first year I returned to teaching, the pond in front of our house had frozen solid. Also, a thick layer of ice hid under five inches of snow in the lane. I didn't really know when I began to slide, but suddenly, there I sat right in the middle of the pond! Horrified, I thought, "What if the ice breaks through? Where are the tractors?" No problem! I eased the car into low gear, glided smoothly off the pond and back into the lane. The old white car behaved beautifully the entire twelve miles of snowy road to Harpers Ferry. Eleven tractor trailers had jackknifed on the once treacherous Alstadt's Hill; my car ploughed on, as if it were apologizing for temporarily inconveniencing me.

Only once have I run out of gas; many times I've come close. In fact, my son voices frequent predictions about how soon it will occur. The time I did was precisely at midnight, but you'd never believe how considerate the car was (the green car, not the white one on the pond). It coughed and sputtered on past darkened residences of people I didn't know, gasped and quit right in front of the home of a familiar, former student. I was so relieved; it would have been humiliating to yell for help in front of a stranger's house at midnight. In just a few moments, my student put his head out the upstairs window (he recognized my hillbilly accent), and exclaimed, "Mrs. Snyder, what in the world are you doing out there this time of night?" Within minutes, he came with a can of gasoline, made a funnel with a piece of cardboard, and had me on my way.

Come to think of it, I don't believe I ever did tell him what I was doing out there that time of night.

Last fall, while driving in the hilly park area of town, I noticed my brakes did nothing at all. Obviously, my psychic vehicle knew I would not have enough common sense to coast toward the curb and cut the ignition. Remembering a filling station about ten (yes, ten!) blocks away, I kept going. Incredible forces went into motion — or rather, *delayed* motion. I still can't believe a car could creep so slowly with so little gas pedal action and not come to a dead stop. Every light I came to was green, even on the left and right angle turns. I dreaded pulling into the filling station because normally, I would be turning against a long line of traffic. Did I? No, not a vehicle was in sight! When my mechanic discovered the master cylinder gone, his shocked expression was, "You mean you drove that far with no brakes?"

He didn't know about my car's protective, psychic powers.

Only once have I totally passed out while driving. I should say "fainted"; "passed out" is too suggestive of another driving problem (not one I would ever have). Evidently, a digestive disorder failed to allow enough oxygen to reach my brain as I neared the railroad crossing on the edge of town. I remember the blackness coming over me. When I became conscious, there my car sat, almost all the way off the highway, two inches from the wire fence, the motor turned off and the transmission in park — super powers at work again!

Also, my cars have possessed an uncanny power to cover themselves with a shield of total invisibility. I'm ashamed to admit I have allowed my inspection stickers to expire more than once or twice. Until a year ago, my cars have kept cruising on, quiet, unseen, cautioning me silently to stay under speed limits, stop at stop signs — to do nothing that might call attention to the paper square in the lower, left corner of the windshield. I believe my car would have backed me up this time if I hadn't been so stupid as to think the flashing lights behind me were warning signals from a vehicle towing a wide load. Under that misconception, I kept on driving for at least an eighth of a mile before I pulled over. I firmly believe that my compassionate car had pleaded with the patrolman not to sound his siren. I knew several people in the community, and they would have been surprised to see me picked up by the police — or would they?

I'm convinced that my cars' protective powers have extended beyond covering mechanical failures; I've never been stopped by an officer of the law who didn't have a sympathetic look on his face!

My driver's license was due for renewal January 1, and rest assured, I didn't forget that. The only fear clouding my declining years that is as strong as having to take another driver's test is an IRS audit!

The first of next month my car license is due (does it ever end?). Unfortunately, the Department of Motor Vehicles ignores the fact that I do not get along well with decals or any other adhesive materials.

You wouldn't believe one of the Christmas gifts from my grandsons — a Super Flat Fixer! I mortified them when I asked if the can contained a substance to spray around the outside of the leak and seal it. The principle of necessary inflation never entered my mind. I reminded them that many "experienced" drivers of my generation would not know what a Super Flat Fixer was!

So — in case of dire circumstances or relentless, creeping years — take away my hair rinse, take away my coral red lipstick, take away my knee socks, take my purple blouse, even my electric blanket — just please don't take my wheels!

The Miracle of the Red Tuxedo

Eight years ago today at 4:00 A.M., a call from the hospital informed me that a new grandson had arrived. Mr. Eric has never done things the easy way. Since he was nearly four weeks late deciding to enter the outside world, his heartbeat had to be carefully monitored throughout labor. Fortunately, it didn't drop lower than twenty beats above the danger line. By then, however, he had stretched his frame until his collar bone was broken in delivery.

When he was sixteen months old, he contracted the worst form of bacterial meningitis. We were told by the doctor, "if he makes it through the night," and "every hour counts." Two week later, thin and weak, he sat on the kitchen sink at home and "mooed" back to the cows in the field outside the window.

At the age of three, he plunged through an upstairs floor register onto a hot wood stove in the room below, missed a steaming iron tea kettle by an inch, branded his hip on the grating of the stove top, and landed on both feet.

His second try at roller skating sent him to the emergency room with a broken arm. Turning too quickly (which he always does), he gashed his cheek on his dad's tool box and informed me later by phone that the doctor told him he was the bravest boy he had sewn up all week (in fact, all year!).

I doubt seriously that I have ever seen him without a bruise, a bump, a skinned place, or a bug bite. Today, there's a red nick on his thigh where I jabbed him with the scissors when I cut off his knee-less jeans to make fringed jams. I don't feel guilty about the wound; it was he who wheedled me into believing it would take too long to pull off his pants over his "sticky" sneakers. Of course removing the "sticky" sneakers would be unthinkable because his older brother had just yelled for him to come play kickball in the yard.

Compared with his peers, Eric is not an "in-between." His eyelashes are longer, his hair straighter, his body skinnier, his voice louder, his temper hotter, his concentration keener and his hugs tighter.

His dad pays him fifty cents a day for watering the calves, a chore he performs not because he especially enjoys it, but because he likes the money for books and Ninja Turtle figures. Steering the tractor, riding in the back of the red pickup (that delight was almost permanently forbidden because he had fallen out twice, once on his head), playing little league, screaming at the Redskins games, hiking the trails of Skyline Drive and tormenting his brother and sister are things he does enjoy.

Right now, he has given up girls for games. When life gets hectic, he retreats to my bedroom, folds back the bedspread, sits cross-legged and plays solitaire. The only time I have even tied his older brother in a game of checkers was when Eric coached me from the sidelines.

He is totally unaware of it, but when I need assurance that there are miracles, all I have to do is look into his big, brown eyes.

On the last day of school this year, he raced down over the hill to tell me (he ran because his bike had a flat tire) he had received the citizenship medal for his room (he had received it in kindergarten and first grade, too), had gotten the second grade library award, straight "A's" the last six weeks and a perfect attendance certificate.

I doubt seriously that his school record made his parental disciplinary measures any less severe when he got in trouble at home that afternoon, but the memory of a miracle can cushion life's little ups and downs for everybody concerned!

He missed his truck ride home for lunch today (had to walk) because we were doing "grown-up talk." He told me he planned to get married young so I'd still be around to go to the wedding — asked if I thought I could hold on 'til he was twenty. We quickly did some mental arithmetic but could not arrive at a definite conclusion.

He also informed me that he planned to be married in a red tuxedo because he never had liked the black and white ones.

I guess when a little person has crammed so much living in a mere eight years, wearing an ordinary tuxedo would be a dull thing to do!

Hannah and I

I think of Hannah often, but yesterday she was constantly on my mind. I did a preliminary inspection of my clothes closets, checking out next season's wearing apparel possibilities, deciding which garments hadn't been worn in so long they could be boxed up and given away.

Hannah and I have been acquainted since the late 1960s, when a pretty, dark-haired student of mine dashed into my classroom one morning to tell me some exciting news. In her grandmother's attic she had found a remarkably well-preserved document that she knew would interest me. It did! It was a two-page, signed and sealed agreement renting a slave by the name of Hannah from the heirs of James Macoughtry, Jr., deceased, to Shenstone Farm from January 1, 1844, until December 25 of the same year. Payment of thirty dollars was to be made by A. C. Timberlake, probably a son of William Timberlake who had purchased Shenstone land in 1796 and shortly after, built the present dwelling.

Checking my rather extensive (but neither elegant nor costly) wardrobe brought Hannah to mind, for I recalled the clearly specified terms of the rental agreement. I pulled the document from a desk drawer and re-read it.

In very legible cursive, it stated that the renter promised to send with Hannah — and I quote — "the following summer clothing, towit:

two new, cotton dresses, two new, cotton chemises, two checked aprons, two cotton handkerchiefs, and a pair of strong, new shoes." The renter (Timberlake) was to return her on Christmas Day with "one homemade, striped, linsey dress of full size, one new chemise, one pair of new, yarn stockings, one blanket of good size, one pair of new, strong shoes, and pay her tax."

The document was signed and sealed by Ephraim and Thomas Watson, Jr., ancestors of the family still well-known in this area.

It's understandable that on this day, I thought of Hannah and contrasted our wardrobes.

Hannah and I have become quite close. She hasn't exactly been a ghost in my house. I haven't seen her materialize on any of the stairway landings, or float like a cloud of vapor through a closed door, but I have felt her presence. She lived in this old house 148 years ago, and in many ways, she is still here.

In the first place, I'm convinced she was special. The Timberlakes paid thirty dollars for her year's rental, and considering the economy of that period, thirty dollars was a handsome sum.

She was not young and inexperienced; the document calls her a servant "woman", not "girl", nor, as was customary, "young female." I'm imagining now — somehow I instinctively know that she was a lady of strong character and worth, and with a kind of regal dignity. I can see her calmly performing her assigned tasks, and without complaints or demands, commanding the respect of her overseers.

So many questions I have asked!

Was she married? I don't think so. I like to think that had she been, the Timberlakes would have rented them as a couple — if they could have afforded to do so.

I wonder what her feelings were as she rode horseback that winter day up the long lane toward the tall, brick house, or perhaps, if her former home had not been too many miles away, as she walked toward the house in her "strong, new shoes." Was she frightened? The Georgian architecture of the house could seem austere and forbidding on a cold, January day.

Often, I've wondered where her new living quarters were. There were slave cabins on the property, in a recessed area of a field east of the house. One chimney still stood like a sentinel guarding the past when my mother-in-law came to Shenstone Farm as a bride in the early 1900s. Or perhaps Hannah was needed close to the house, and consequently, was put in one of the attic rooms. They were spacious, and both had a small window on each side of the chimney, but she would have been so hot in summer and so cold in winter. Maybe the chimneys, even without a fireplace opening, would have retained some of the warmth from the downstairs fires when the cold north wind blew.

I've wondered what her duties were.

Did she cook in the kitchen built in the yard apart from the house? If so, on chilly, fall days, did she have a shawl to drape around her shoulders when she carried food in the covered dishes along the stone walkway into the dining room of the big house? In zero weather, did she simmer pork stew in an iron pot in the oversize fireplace of the southeast, brick-floored, basement room? She might have used the same cast iron crane that still hangs inside the fireplace.

I'm sure she did outside work also. No doubt she went to the garden for potatoes, onions, asparagus, squash, corn, and certainly for a variety of herbs. Possibly, she had helped with the planting and the hoeing.

When crop deadlines faced the owners, she might have accompanied the men to the fields to cradle the wheat and bind it into sheaves, or later in fall, to shuck the ears of corn on the seasoned fodder shocks before the first snowfall.

I can't really know what her chores were, but for some unexplainable reason, I believe her principal duty was to care for the children in the household. Maybe she took them with her to gather eggs in the nearby hen house, allowing them to trail along beside her and to feel the warmth of the freshly-laid egg seconds after the hen cackled and flew from the nest. She probably scolded them when they chased the guinea fowl just to hear them clamor, "Pod-e-rac! Pod-e-rac!"

The children might have played near her in the yard while she scrubbed the clothes with lye soap on the washboard. She would constantly caution them about the boiling water in the cavernous, iron kettle and about the hot, locust embers underneath.

Maybe in mid-summer when Hannah sat on the kitchen steps preparing vegetables for the bountiful noonday meal, one curious child would notice a slim, green shoot peeping through the ground, and Hannah would explain to the child that the plant would some day grow into a tall, black walnut tree. On winter nights, a family would sit in front of a glowing fireplace and crack the nuts with a hammer on a heavy anvil.

Even yet, in the old house there are tales of a spinning wheel whirring at midnight in the same basement room where Hannah cooked. Could it be that long after folks had gone to bed and the house had settled for the night, Hannah sat and spun wool and flax into linsey dresses and petticoats for her mistress' family? If there is a spinning wheel ghost, I hope it is Hannah!

I wonder if she had any time that was hers alone. Did she ever sing, "Nobody knows the trouble I see, Nobody knows but Jesus?" in a low, mournful key, or did she entertain the children with an exciting rendition of "Ezekiel saw the wheel, way up in the middle of the air?" In late evening, did she ever have moments free to walk in the fields and watch the sun go down, or to search for the noisy bullfrog down on the pond bank, or to help the children catch a firefly and put it in a jar?

Most of all, I suppose, I wonder what happened to her after Christmas Day of 1844. Maybe she was such a trusted, congenial worker that the Timberlakes rented her for another year.

I do know that the following year the farm went up for sale. The notice was published:

"For Sale — 1846 — Shenstone — a commodious brick dwelling of three stories, with wide hall, thirteen-foot ceilings, hand-carved wains-coating, and a colonial doorway with fan-lighted arch."

Where was Hannah when the Timberlakes packed up their belongings and left the farm?

I can't believe she ever left Shenstone. Often now, at night, I hear the dry boards on the stairway creak. It could be Hannah creeping quietly down the attic stairs, checking to see if the children are covered up and if all the candles have been snuffed out.

Do I Have To?

The word "adapt" is a powerful word. To adapt is more than to accept. To accept is to take it like it is — don't fight — step back! To adapt conjures up a feeling of subtle comfort after a slight struggle, after trimming off the edges of a thorny situation.

I always prided myself as an adapter — not as dramatically effective as the three-pronged, electric current conductor that dictates drastic changes in the use of appliances, but yes, I could adapt. I knew nothing about being a dairy farmer's wife, but I adapted; granted, I simply stopped trying to be one. My teaching career centered around senior high school, but recently I appeared before an awards assembly of grades one through six. Admittedly, I spent two full days on a ten-minute talk — far more than I used to spend on an entire week's lesson plans in high school — but I could adapt — until today!

Last night I arrived at my daughter's home in Alabama. Nearly a year ago I had spent three weeks here with her family and felt assured that getting settled in this year would pose no problem. All I had to adapt to last night was re-learning the location of the night light and the nearest bathroom.

Today, however, was different. Early this morning the front porch was flooded with the southern sunlight I had flown eight hundred miles to enjoy. I stepped outside to walk in its warmth.

Modern storm door latches are true marvels; they are made to keep in whom and what you want to keep in and to (without question) keep out whom and what you want to keep out. However, door latches cannot compensate for human error. If you accidentally kick your grandson's muddy sneaker between the door and the sill, the latch fails to function.

When I returned a half hour later, I found the door four inches ajar. Baby, one of the calmest house cats I know, had disappeared into the unknown countryside. Hopefully, he will come home before the family does.

I consoled myself by reasoning it was too early in the season for the house to be invaded by a swarm of flying insects, but my knowledge of the roaming habits of the cottonmouth was not sufficient for me to feel secure.

A year ago I enjoyed my leisurely luncheons at my daughter's house. My cooking facilities had included stoves fired by Kentucky coal, locust wood, dirty oil burners and electricity, but not propane gas. Potatoes are a basic in my limited medical diet, so I tried them on the gas burner. Quick heat sent the liquid foaming down the sides of the pot and the sputtering flames leaping skyward. I frantically cut the gas supply back, only to wonder minutes later how something that simmers can scorch.

I shudder to think of what my poached egg will be like at supper time. It's a diet requirement, too.

Don't think I'm downing cooking with gas. I just hadn't "adapted."

Previously, I had suggested that Beth purchase canned green beans for me because they were tender, only required heating — and a can opener. After the potato episode, I felt confident I could regulate the gas flame, but what about the can opener? There it reclined on the wall, proclaiming to me with its beady, red light that it was primed and ready for use. Not by me! I couldn't even get it off the wall! What made me feel so defeated was that last year I did learn to get it off the wall; I just couldn't get it to open a can.

I had obviously regressed in my ability to "adapt."

Time came for ice in my drink. With my glass I pushed the back pedal of the ice maker — evidently too far — much too far! The protruding pedal stuck, shooting an endless cascade of ice cubes all over the kitchen floor. In desperation, and fearful of falling amid the miniature icebergs, I slid the front lever to the adjacent stop. Water gushed out in torrents, streamed across the floor, pausing only to saturate the paper bags of dog and cat food in the pantry. The printed labels on the front of the maker listed water, crushed ice and ice cubes; nothing told me to take my forefinger and pull the pedal forward if it got stuck.

Beth left the stereo system on for me this morning — so I could truly relax. Carefully, she had pointed out to me all the black rectangles and squares that triggered the tape deck, the radio, the TV, assuring me that depressing one particular rectangle would shut down the entire operation.

After enjoying a Kenny Rodgers video, I decided I was relaxed enough for an afternoon nap. I pushed every black object in the entire unit — over and over again — and nothing happened. From last year I remembered the volume control, primarily because it required sliding rather than pushing.

As I quietly left the room, the mass of ebony, geometric figures sneered at me as if to say, "You don't adapt very well, do you?"

Before lying down I wearily returned to the kitchen. In view of my lack of mechanical aptitude and my defective up-close vision, I knew I'd need my bifocals to adjust the ceiling fan in my bedroom!

I like a warm bath when I wake up. Would I dare try the hot tub in the master bedroom? No way! When I was a child, a bath in the galvanized wash tub on Saturday night was the highlight of the week. How could I be expected to adapt to a progress cycle that spans from that ritual to a hot tub? The only whirlpool we enjoyed was when Mother added hot water out of the blue-speckled teakettle spout!

Also, I haven't forgotten the trouble I had a year ago adjusting to the single faucet on the bathtub because both the hot and the cold water poured through the same spout — and isn't it utterly ridiculous that one round, plastic knob regulates both the water temperature and the flow?

Does it drain the water too? Right now, I can't remember —

Adapt? Is it really so essential? Couldn't we who are — shall I say "growing older?" — be allowed to stop trying so hard to adapt and simply *persevere*?

I know I can do that!

Beyond all Boundaries

No Boundaries
Oceanside, California

Yesterday, I believe my two grandchildren (Jimmy, eight, and Martha, six) were a bit surprised when the roaming mummy on the set of Universal Studios in Hollywood hugged me first; I assured them he honored me first because I was nearer his own age, and in many respects, more similar in form!

The whole day at the Studios was fantastic. I've been a film fan ever since Sylvia Sydney, Henry Fonda, and Fred MacMurray made the first technicolor movie "The Trail of the Lonesome Pine" in the 1930s. The Universal lot impressed me because it is not merely a reproduction nor a re-creation; it is an enormous working set where movie and television production never stops.

Why wouldn't a retired English teacher thrill to walk on a street setting lifted directly from the pages of Dickens' England? It was so easy to imagine Sydney Carton, lonely and unkempt, slouched at a corner table of the Pub.

Yes, yesterday was both a fun and learning experience, and I won't forget it — but it could be that what I experienced today will be even more sharply etched in my memory.

My daughter's family and I were guests at a small wedding held in a sandstone gazebo on the shores of the Pacific. Huge boulders, some pushed up by winter storms, formed a natural arena, and trellised purple phlox produced a spectacular backdrop for the columns of the gazebo. The ocean breezes were cool, but they were still tempered by the warmth of the afternoon sun.

Music wasn't needed for the wedding. There was so much rhythm in the tide as the giant waves lapped upon the shore and broke into white, staccato swirls.

Ann, the bride's mother, had helped my son-in-law with French when he was getting his doctorate in pathology at Duke University.

Mary, the bride, was lovely — tall, slender, graceful. Her jet black hair was center-parted, braided, and double-coiled down her back. Surprisingly, her dress was much like my own late 1940s wedding dress — sheath style, mid-calf length, with a ruffled peplun around the waist. Right before the ceremony, she donned a small pillbox hat with a veil that covered her eyes.

The bridegroom, straight and slim, was striking in his tux — oyster white in color like her dress — both people quietly and tastefully elegant.

The above details could describe many marriage ceremonies, and I suppose quite a few wedding vows have been exchanged at sunset along seashores, but the characters in this group stand out.

Ann, the bride's mother, is a Quaker lady, who had years ago married a Chinese professor of languages. To them were born three children. After her husband died and she had retired from teaching, Ann moved to Hawaii, purchased three acres of rich land and began to raise Plymouth Rock hens. She doesn't sell the chickens; she sells the huge, brown eggs for (she says) a "premium price."

In Mary, the gorgeous bride, genetics seemed to mold the softest, loveliest features of both races, not only in appearance but in mannerisms — in the way her eyes smile, the way she hears your every word.

And the bridegroom? Sylvester is a black Marine, has been in the service for ten years. His friendly, caring manner made it easy to see why Ann with her pacifist leanings could welcome this gentle military man into her daughter's life.

There was a preliminary ritual for Ann to perform. She had brought several leis from Hawaii, had made them herself, and had stored them so carefully that in color and essence they were as fresh as the day she wove them. The bride's and groom's leis were made of jasmine. Orchids went to Loki (the bride's sister and matron of honor), also to Loki's skilled, Vermont cabinetmaker husband and their bright-eyed, baby daughter.

The sun was dropping low over the Pacific when Ann gently draped the leis over the heads of the wedding party. I thought, "What a wonderful way to bind together — what a symbol of love!"

Above the sound of the breeze and the waves, we could easily hear the words the lady minister read — promises the two had written to each other. A Quaker lady, a Chinese-Caucasian bride, a black bridegroom in the Military — I looked out at the vast Pacific, watched daylight fade and moonlight begin to shimmer on the water, and I *knew* that something far bigger than race or creed or color or human frailty, or even human greatness, is out there. I knew that each of us in our own inimitable way is a part of that infinity.

No longer could we tell where the sea met the sky. I remember the fleeting revelation, "How small we are!" But instead of feeling overwhelmed and threatened by what lay beyond that sheet of silver, I felt warm, safe, sheltered.

Somehow I knew that what we have been, still are, and can be on this earth will carry us beyond all boundaries of land, sky, or sea!

To Live Is to Learn

Seventy years ago on a snowy January day, a young man and a young lady stood in the middle of a railroad crossing in the hills of eastern Kentucky. The young man had a job hauling poplar timber down from the mountains with a mule team; the young lady taught in a one-room school, forty pupils in eight grades, and was paid one dollar per pupil, per month.

They were waiting to be married. The preacher was a coal miner and he had promised to come outside the nearby mine during his lunch hour to marry them. He came — his face black with coal dust. He took a small Bible from his metal lunch box and performed the ceremony without removing his cap with the carbide lamp jutting out in front.

The couple built a modest, three-room, plank house alongside a creek, and over a period of years three daughters were born to them. The father left his hauling job to work as a storekeeper for the railroad in the nearby town; he ordered parts for the steam locomotives. The mother stopped teaching to care for her home and her family.

When the oldest daughter was in second grade in the mining camp school, her beautiful, and usually reasonable, teacher told the class to — in one night — memorize the first two pages of Longfellow's poem "Hiawatha" — a lovely poem but full of unfamiliar Indian names. The mother and daughter labored long into the night until the little girl had mastered the two pages.

Next morning, however, when she stood before the class to recite, she felt panic sweeping over her. Only one line could she remember -"By the shining big sea Water stood the wigwam of Nokomis." Tears came as she walked back to her desk.

After school, tears fell again when she told her mother about the poem. Her mother put both arms around her and said gently, "Don't cry. You did the best you could."

A few years later all three daughters were given second-hand bicycles; their dad could fix anything, so he had them in excellent condition — but the oldest child had never been well coordinated. In sports, no matter how hard she tried, she was awkward and clumsy. The sisters could even ride out on the county road or on the cinder path along the railroad track, but the oldest couldn't.

One day, noting her distress, her mother said, "Sit down a minute. I want to tell you a story, or it's really a little poem by a man named Emerson.

"It's about a mountain and a squirrel. The mountain was always making fun of the little squirrel. He bragged, 'Look, I can carry trees on my back.' The little squirrel got tired of being ridiculed. Finally, he said to the mountain, 'Listen, Big Boy, if I cannot carry forests on my back, neither can you crack a nut!' "

Then the mother added, "See, nobody can do everything; we each can do different things. Don't expect too much of yourself."

In seventh grade the oldest daughter made the finals in the spelling bee that determined who went to the county seat twenty-five miles away for the big spelling contest. She had always had trouble with the word "necessary," always added a second "c." The big day came. Only she and a boy classmate were still standing. The teacher pronounced the word — yes, it was "necessary," and, yes, she added a second "c."

When she got home and told her mother that Adrian had won the match, her mother said quietly, "Honey, you did the best you could. We can't always be first."

However, her grades were good, and she was named valedictorian of the eighth-grade graduating class (schools then were on a one-to-eight and a nine-to-twelve system).

She loved her new, white crepe dress with the button-on cape that her parents had bought her for the graduation exercises, but oh, how she longed for a pair of silk stockings! Ribbed cotton would never look right with that pretty, white dress.

On the morning of her graduation, her mother walked a mile down the railroad track, boarded the ten o'clock passenger train and rode into town four miles away. Waiting all day after buying the silk stockings was tiring, but she couldn't get another train home until four o'clock.

That night, as the daughter started to put on the new dress, her mother walked into the room and handed her the tan, silk stockings. "We want you to know we're proud of you," she said, and the daughter saw tears in her mother's eyes.

High school posed a few problems though. When the daughter was in tenth grade, she hesitated when she handed the first six-weeks' report card to her mother. In all subjects but math there were "A's." Math was not just a plain "C;" it was a "C" followed by a minus sign! The girl waited nervously. Then she heard, "In math, did you do the best you could?" She had to tell the truth — at least almost. She couldn't quite admit that she had a terrible crush on the boy who sat across from her, and if her mind hadn't kept wandering, she could have made at least a "B." Almost as if her mother read her thoughts, she just said, "I know math is hard for you. Maybe you can bring it to a 'B' next time," — and she did (no minus either); but not once all during high school did she ever make an "A" in math.

Somehow she knew her mother didn't expect her to.

A close friend of the daughter became the high school valedictorian; the daughter ranked second. She was afraid her parents would be disappointed because after all, she had been valedictorian in the eighth grade. On graduation night she was so shocked to hear her name called for the Citizenship Award. On the way home that night, her mother said, "Your daddy and I think the Citizenship medal is just about the highest honor anyone can get!"

On the day her oldest daughter graduated from college, her mother gave her some advice that she never forgot — "Honey, don't ever stop learning; that's when you stop living!"

The oldest daughter went out on her own, but there were two more girls to send to college. The father had a steady job, but his pay would not send two at the same time. The mother thought, "If only I could go back to teaching!" — but how? Yes, she had taught years before, but a new law required two years of college for a teaching certificate. She didn't even have a high school diploma; in fact, she had never even been to high school. Years ago, she had simply attended a summer institute, had taken a test, and become a teacher.

Early one summer morning she boarded the bus for the county seat. Only her husband knew why she was going; I doubt that she herself was sure where or to whom she was going — but two weeks later, a temporary certificate, allowing her to teach grades one through six arrived in the mail. Her salary was less, but that amount, along with the father's pay, sent two girls through college.

Naturally, she would stop teaching then. No, she didn't. Every weekday morning she walked up the road to the mining camp school. Quite often the family supper was late because she stayed after school to give special help to a child with a learning problem.

It seemed no time at all until she was teaching her grandchildren.

The years passed quickly. Even after she retired from teaching, she tutored slow children on weekends and did all kinds of community work.

She really didn't retire from teaching — certainly not from learning!

One October she went back into the hills along the old logging road and gathered a dozen different kinds of leaves. She laid the leaves on cloth of the same rich, fall colors, cut around them, then stitched the bright cloth leaves onto squares of white. She named her quilt "Autumn," and gave it to the grandson who bore her husband's name. Another October came — the hills aflame in gold and crimson. She was tired that week; she had hosted her Homemakers' Club, presenting a program on quick desserts and serving samples.

A few nights later, she and her partner of forty-nine years sat in the living room. While he waited for the ball scores on television, she read aloud to him the skit she had prepared for the local Parent Teacher Association. They laughed together — the PTA dads had agreed to do a mock wedding (all male) if she would write the dialogue.

Not long after they had gone to bed, he heard her sigh, and she was gone — no struggle, no pain.

They buried her in a little family cemetery on the hillside — surrounded by pines that look tall enough to brush the sky. It's so quiet up there — so quiet you can hear the creek gurgling down below, the wind whispering in the pine trees, and the faint, far-away sound of a bob-white calling for his mate.

I don't know what is inscribed on the tombstone. I've seen it, but I don't remember. I know what could be written:

"She lived to Learn, and in doing so, she Taught so many!"

That lady was my mother.

Guess who the little girl was who never learned to ride a bicycle and who never once made an "A" in math!

Allergies and Pet Peeves

More than once, my allergy doctors have asked, "Do you live in an old house?"

"Around one hundred ninety years old."

"Do you live near a corn field?"

"Surrounded by them."

"Are you bothered by weather changes?"

"If St. Peter should call and ask what I'd like Heaven to be like, I'd tell him if the temperature could stay between eighty and ninety-two, I could handle anything else." I wouldn't dare request a higher temperature; he might recommend I take up residence elsewhere.

All along, my doctors have assured me that allergies seldom kill. Mine could.

I'm not often irritable (honest!). For me, living is fun. My lackluster days are few. However, if I continue to be as miserable as I was yesterday, I won't have to wait for my allergies to kill me. Some well-meaning loved one will probably beat them to it.

All day in spite of my throbbing head, scratchy throat and drippy nose, I've kept telling myself, "Keep going. Act normal."

Naturally, eating was essential. But first, I had to take my mild digestive pill for my IBS (new, fancy term for my other ailment that won't kill me).

I got out the bottle, pressed forcefully down on the cap with the palm of my hand, turned, pushed again, turned again. Nothing happened. Then, realizing the top resembled the cap on my grandfather's highly alcoholic cough elixir of fifty years ago, I cautiously unscrewed the top in one motion! Could it be we are going "simple" again!

To economize, I had begun to buy my decaffeinated soda in large, plastic bottles. Problem was, I had to use a wet dish cloth to get enough traction to unscrew the top, but the "fizz" had long since evaporated into thin air.

Meanwhile, someone had left the back porch screen ajar, and several flies had sought warmer temperatures inside. I got out my new can of insect spray guaranteed to kill anything with wings. It might have — if it had sprayed. Thank goodness I had not trashed my old, green, rubber fly swatter with the warped, wire handle.

I decided to read my new household magazine. I was unable to read the magazine; I was wrestling with it! Every half dozen pages, a cardboard insert would pop up. I tolerated the ad for subscription renewal, but the porcelain-dolls, new-fabric-softener-sample and fifty cents-off-salad-dressing inserts — please!!

Then I remembered that soothing music always calms me. At a local department store, I recently purchased a cassette of famous waltzes (even "Blue Danube", and "The Merry Widow"). The tape was entombed in one of those long, white, three-sectioned cases. Right now, it's lying useless on top of, not inside, my tape deck.

I'd like to gripe more about my pet peeves, but the pen I paid $1.79 for is gradually fading.

If St. Peter should call about my heavenly requests, I won't mention my allergies, not even my preference for hot weather. I'll plead, "Could you stock up on spray cans that spray and sodas that are permanently carbonated? One more request, since nobody steals in Heaven, could you please remove my favorite cassettes from their tombs and stack them on an open shelf? I'd be eternally grateful!"

Lest We Forget

Seldom do I find what I'm searching for in my attic — but yesterday I did.

My seventh-grade grandson and I had been discussing the Persian Gulf War, and I knew there were things I wanted him to see. I found them, in an oversized, brown envelope, lying in the drawer of an antique dressing table that had been propped against the chimney because one leg was missing.

There they were — the mementoes of World War II, when I, just out of college, taught in a large, consolidated senior high school in the hills of eastern Kentucky. There lay photographs (all black and white, of course), letters, insignia, a pressed orchid corsage with powdery edges, and other interesting items. Many souvenirs were from students; their names came easily.

Bill, the tall, black-haired class Lothario, had written from Germany to thank me for the Christmas "frutcake" I had sent him — Bill had always considered it a waste of time to include a silent letter when he spelled a word. Greg was an orphan and never had a steady girl friend, so he sent me his corporal stripes when he made sergeant. Troy had sent a folder of post cards (some a bit risque`) from post-war Tokyo.

One article, a crisp, yellow telegram, made me laugh aloud. Too many World War II telegrams did not evoke laughter; this one did.

It had been sent to me by my red-haired boy friend from Jacksonsville, Florida, where he was enrolled in Officers' Candidate School. When I planned a train trip, I felt confident that my dad was sure I was going to Miami to visit my girl friend in the WAVES (and I was — but not directly!). I can still hear Daddy when he brought home the telegram that had unfortunately been delivered to him at the railroad office where he worked. The wire read, "No hotel rooms available in Jacksonsville. Come on and share park bench."

Previously, J.P.'s sense of humor was one characteristic that appealed to me — but not that day! All that saved me was the fact that the word "rooms" had an "s" on the end. That experience taught me in teaching grammar to appreciate the importance of the plural!

However, two pieces of paper in the brown envelope mattered most.

One afternoon when I checked roll in my last period English class, I noticed Daryl's chair was empty. Daryl would be easily missed; not only was he the Pirates' star basketball player, he was also an honor student. When I inquired about him, a friend said, "Oh, didn't you know, Miss Stanley? He left for the Navy this morning."

The letter I found yesterday was sent from Guadalcanal a few weeks later. It was a newsy letter with warm, personal overtones, significantly signed, "Yours for a better world, Daryl."

Daryl did make this a better world. On the GI bill he went to college and then on to medical school. Today he is a busy surgeon in a sizable, southern town. His medical complex is modern and his facilities sophisticated, but people from far away clay hills travel hundreds of miles to have him operate on themselves and on their loved ones. They come, not only because he accepts Medicare assignments, but because they know he combines skill with compassion.

The promise Daryl made on a Guadalcanal battleground has been kept — he has made this a better world.

Destiny, however, took a different turn with Rob.

Tucked down in the corner of the brown envelope was a special type of memorabilia. Shocked, I realized it was a faded but uncrumpled V-mail letter — that breakthrough of the 1940s, the common man's introduction to terms such as "photostatic" and "microfilm". So much could be said on a tiny wisp of paper. Rob did say so much.

Rob was a friend all through high school, and he was still my friend when I returned from college to teach. I noticed that still his buddies teased him because he was a direct descendant of Randall McCoy of Hatfield-McCoy feud fame, but there had never lived a gentler soul!

In our high school math classes, he was a whiz kid, but oh, how he detested English! He helped me with geometry and I tutored him in literature. It took me days to coach him in memorizing the five stanzas of Kipling's "Recessional." I can still hear his triumphant shout from the post office steps (his mother was postmistress in the mining camp) when he finally perfected the memorization — proclaiming loudly and clearly the chorus lines, "Lord God of Hosts, be with us yet, lest we forget — lest we forget!"

When war came, he volunteered and climbed fast, excelling as a navigator. He wrote often. The V-mail letter I found yesterday had faded, but I could still decipher the closing "Lord God of Hosts, be with us yet, Lest we forget! — Rob."

On the back of the letter, pale but still discernible, stamped in black type, was the phrase "Missing in Action".

Rob's was the first U.S. war plane to go down over the North Sea in World War II.

Will I show the contents of the brown envelope to my 12-year-old grandson? Yes! When I do, I will attempt to assure him that in any war, many, like Daryl, will return to make a better world, but on the other hand, some, like Rob, will not come home. I plan to remind my grandson, however, that Rob died assuring us there is a higher power, a "Lord of our far-flung battle line, Lord God of Hosts" who will help us overcome those described in Kipling's poem as being "drunk with the sight of power."

I want my grandson to love his country, but — like me — to hate the concept of war, to be baffled by it, terrified of it; at the same time, I want him to hold sacred the memories of the Daryls and the Robs.

Hopefully, their stories will inspire him and his generation to not abandon the quest for the heretofore elusive secret of lasting peace.

Never Too Old To Learn

Every time I visited Jim on the dairy farm before we were married, I tried hard to convince him that a Kentucky school teacher would make an ideal dairy farmer's wife. I would even go out and sit on the wooden feedbox in the stable and marvel at how efficiently he could hook up the milkers and go through each step of the process. My, how strong he was to lift those heavy, ten-gallon, metal cans up off the floor and into the milk tank — all in one single motion! My heart skipped several beats!

Actually, the old-time stables could be rather romantic despite their poor aromatic quality. Unless there were too many kickers in the herd, there was a hush not present in today's noisy, automated, assembly line milking parlor.

But I think Jim knew even then that I would never be an asset to his primary source of income. In fact, not long after we were married, I slipped quietly into the stable one morning to relay a message. Almost frantically, he whispered, "Dess, get out of here as soon as you can! That old white cow goes crazy when you're around!"

I later wondered if he had trained her to do precisely that!

I don't dislike cows; I'm not at all afraid of them; a field of grazing cattle adds new depth to the meaning of the word "pastoral"; they rank high on my list of favorite animals; I just can't think of any constructive thing to do when I'm around them.

And then I became inspired; if I couldn't impress Jim with my dairy expertise in the barn, I could in the kitchen — with dairy *products.* I certainly would not squander my time on ordinary projects like whipping cream or churning butter. Besides, the glass Daisy churn was down in the cellar covered with cobwebs and full of spiders. I knew what I would do — I would make cottage cheese!

Even today, my family and closest friends cannot believe I ever once succeeded.

I knew the pan of milk had to be set in a warm place. Jim's mother used to set the vessel on the hot water reservoir of her Home Comfort stove (perfect!). When the already skimmed milk aged to a couple of degrees beyond sour and thickened (we called this stage "clabber" in Kentucky), I would test it by sticking my forefinger in it and pressing down. If the curved dent remained, it was ready to cook — except you didn't *cook* it. You didn't even simmer it. The process on an early vintage electric burner with only low, medium and high controls was tricky. However, if it happened to be my lucky day, the whey would push to the top of the pan, and there on the bottom would be soft, pulpy chunks of cheese (comparable to today's commercial large curd). But if during the heating process, I had to change a diaper, or had stayed out in the yard twenty seconds too long hanging sheets on the line, or had carelessly allowed the temperature of the clabber to rise two degrees too quickly — I could never understand why the resulting spongy mass took on a greenish hue!

I'm glad Jim's pigs did not object to the color of their supper delicacy; they consumed it far more frequently than we did!

Looking back, I'm sure Jim knew all along that I would eventually realize I didn't need to impress him by sharing his occupational interests (he had hoped so, anyway!) and would return to the classroom where I was when he met me.

Teaching and milking blended beautifully, especially in our supper table talk. By far the best news he ever shared with me was that my sworn enemy, the white cow, had begun losing her temper with everyone else. I had thought her bovine animosity toward me might have been kindled by my red hair, but that theory was dispelled after she butted my brother-in-law into the drainage trough and nearly dislocated Jim's shoulder during the same milking session. I shed no tears when she was carted off to the stock sale the following Monday, but the person who bid the highest on her had my deepest sympathy.

After the installation of the milking parlor, and after I had mysteriously developed a total allergy to all dairy products (my allergist assured me the problem was chemical and not psychological), I felt less guilty about my meager contributions to the farm.

However, all through the years, there was one dairy-related skill Jim had hoped I would master. The duty would not have interfered with my teaching because it was nocturnal.

During all forty-three of the years I've lived on Shenstone farm, the field right below the house has been designated as the "birthing lot" (almost always used when outdoor temperatures hovered around zero). Cows with nursing babies and those periodically desiring romance were kept in other lots nearby.

My hearing was keener than Jim's, and I know that life would have been less hectic for him if I had learned to differentiate between the mournful call of a mama cow whose baby bull calf had been sold that morning, the repetitious wail of a prospective lover, or the groan of one in the throes of a difficult labor.

Many times I woke Jim in the night and declared the cow I heard was, without the slightest doubt, in the final stage of labor, only to be quietly informed, "Oh, she had her calf this morning. We put it in the pen, and she's bawling for it."

Before I could venture to ask, "Why didn't you tell me?" he'd be fast asleep.

A week or so later I would nudge him again, and he would patiently say, "That's just Number Ninety-Two who" — shall I say it daintily? "wants to be bred."

Some nights, thinking surely I'd be right once, he would light his lantern, trudge through the snowy field, return shortly and tell me, "I never heard a sound out of any of them."

Then — this morning, forty-three years after I sat on the feedbox for the first time — I redeemed myself! I made up for all the former miscalculations.

After his dad passed away four years ago, our son Nick desperately needed to "sound-train" me because he lived up on the hill two wide fields away — out of earshot of the moans and groans — lucky guy!

At 4:30 this morning I heard a cow. A lament? A love call? Moans? I debated a half hour, decided on the latter, and called Nick.

Within minutes I saw truck lights go down the lane, turn, and beam into the "birthing lot" — then a pause — then truck lights returning fast up the lane on to the supply shed. Nick had come for a rope.

The rope didn't make me cringe. I had learned that when a rope is gently wrapped around the front legs down near the hoofs, the baby is eager to be free and probably ignores any possible discomfort — see, I'm not completely ignorant about the dairy!

In the meantime, I had put on my robe, gone down into the kitchen and turned on the back porch light.

Before too long, Nick came in. As he washed his hands, he remarked with a touch of wonder in his voice, "You actually got it right this time. It's a big bull calf, and he couldn't have made it by himself. Remind me to give you a cut when I sell him."

He wasn't referring to an edible "cut."

I'll bet Jim would have been proud of me!

One Sentence Can Say So Much

Kinds of Sentences: Declarative,
Interrogative,
Exclamatory,
Imperative

Many times during my teaching career I wrote the above on the blackboard in my Palmer method penmanship. Notice I still say "blackboard". I remained too traditional (or obstinate) to refer to the teaching tool as a "chalkboard," even after many surfaces turned to green.

But this is not a grammar lesson. I want merely to emphasize the power and scope of a single sentence in any of the above classifications — not a paragraph nor a page — just one sentence, either written or spoken.

I vividly recall the first sentence my husband ever wrote to me. Supposedly, I had come to Jefferson County from Kentucky to visit a dear friend, but seeing her, I'll admit, was not my only intention. I came, knowing she had an eligible, bachelor brother who admired horses, flowers and redheads, not necessarily in that order. My visit to the farm extended significantly beyond my previously planned departure date. Of course, back in the 1940s, the girl never wrote first, nor called, nor asked for a date, nor met in a hotel without a chaperone, nor even hinted at a proposal, etc. So, as was socially acceptable, I returned to Kentucky, allowed a reasonable number of days for mail to travel 460 miles, then began a daily mile-long trek down the railroad track to the post office. The letter was not long in coming.

The first sentence was, "It certainly has been quiet around here since you left."

Did he mean quiet as in "I missed you," or (hopefully not) as in "The farm has been so peaceful since you left"?

Since the letters continued to come and the opening sentences became less ambiguous and more thrilling, I concluded he missed me.

A few years later a single sentence rang down the curtain on an extremely tense drama in my life.

My body did not tolerate pregnancies well; physically, I was not made for motherhood. I spent five weeks in the hospital before our son was born (cost per week — one-hundred dollars!). However, after all the anxiety and possible danger, he entered the world in a normal fashion, leaving all of us relieved and proud.

With the second pregnancy, though, problems multiplied. At the end of the seventh month, the surgeon was forced to remove three tumors, discovering when he did, alarming signs of malignancy. Thankfully, that threat tested negative, but fearing the return of the blood tumors, the doctor planned a Caesarean at the end of the eighth month. Questions hung like clouds over us. Had pressure from the fist-size tumors damaged the fetus? Since I had lost rather than gained weight during the pregnancy, would the premature baby be large enough to survive? Would the faulty vascular system continue to pose a threat?

What the surgeon did on a September morning, exactly one month before the due date, bordered on the spectacular. He found it necessary (still fearing cancer) to perform a three-in-one — a Caesarean, a hysterectomy and a bladder lift, all in one session — truly a major medical undertaking forty years ago! Having been given a spinal, I lay completely aware of all that was being done, could hear every word that was said, and could plainly see the lighted incubator six feet to my right.

When the doctor lifted the baby by her ankles and she squalled lustily, he uttered a sentence I'll never forget, "There's not one thing wrong with this baby!"

Instantly, I fell into a deep (and, I think, deserved) sleep and didn't know for hours that the incubator was never needed. She weighed over six pounds and was fully developed except for the paleness of her fingernails. I'm sure my doctor needed sleep, too!

One sentence can demonstrate what forgiveness is all about.

While teaching English one day, I wrongfully accused a boy of cheating on an exam. Evidence, though circumstantial, pointed strongly toward his guilt, but I failed to check out the facts. Later in the day I discovered I had been totally mistaken. When I called him out of a fellow teacher's last period class, he walked toward me, wary and unsmiling. There was no easy way to apologize except to call him by his name and say, "I made a terrible mistake, and I am so sorry." A long moment of silence — then I'll never forget what the young man did and said. First, he put out his hand, then quietly said "I know you didn't mean me no harm, Mrs. Snyder."

His grammar wasn't good but his heart was. He taught me in one sentence and a handshake the true meaning of forgiveness.

Often the sharpest and possibly the most constructive reprimand can be expressed in a very brief sentence. One of my children used that method to open my eyes and teach me a powerful lesson. During an emotional time in our family, when my behavioral attitudes were intolerant and narrow, when my thinking had become totally fogged in by the age-old question, "What will people say?", my child confronted me with five words, "Mom, you of all people!" So much can be pressed into that short, bombastic statement — not all condemnation, not all disillusionment —

but when others, particularly those who know us well, tell us we are acting in a manner below their expectations, we begin to reassess and to re-evaluate our thinking. I know I did!

The thermometer doesn't say "spring" today, but I know it's here. Lately a playful Mother Nature has enjoyed a teasing game with the new grass venturing above ground in the yard and fields, turning it to green with warm, gentle rains, back to brown again with nippy winds and snow blankets, but today it looks as if the green has caught hold and is here to stay. My grandson agreed when he dropped in after school. His first words when he entered the kitchen door were, "Grandma, there's a whole new world out there!" That happens to be one of my favorite single sentences.

One more sentence I must mention. Not long ago after something wonderful and special had happened to me — just one of many mountaintop experiences — a close friend made a beautiful statement. She told me, "Dess, I'll declare, it just seems the stars shine down upon you!"

From that exclamation came an idea.

I really don't want an inscription on my tombstone — please not "Her Trials and Tribulations are over," not even "Gone but not forgotten." If, however, someone insists that a memorial be carved, I would prefer: "The Stars Shone down upon Her and She Was Grateful!"

Even an appropriate epitaph can be meaningfully etched in a single sentence!

Where We Live And Who We Are

It's late Sunday evening. I'm not planning to watch the news on television tonight; I don't want to break the spell.

Not often do I remain out of circulation for two full weeks. In an attempt to overpower a head infection and to confine my misery to myself, I had stayed away from people, except, of course, for my routine visits to the beauty shop. No doubt that is why today I especially needed people and craved contact with my nearby village.

I realize many believe we should be reverently silent from the moment we enter a church sanctuary. I respect their beliefs, and I was silent when I stood inside St. Anne's Basilica in Canada, and when I entered other places of worship, but if I were quiet in the time period before my own church service begins, there would be so much I wouldn't learn — whose surgery was not as radical as expected, whose daughter was bringing the new baby home for a visit, yes, my young friend would make me a coconut pound cake to store in the freezer for company, and no, my head wasn't back to normal. There would be a chuckle about that announcement, and most likely, one of the fellows would quip, "When was your head ever normal?"

This morning, when the musical prelude began, I settled, except during the first hymn, I did whisper to my close friend in front of me,

"Your hubby surely looks classy in that gray suit!"

Morning sunlight streamed through the splendid, stained glass windows. Isn't it a pity that today's inflated prices have made reproducing such beauty totally prohibitive?

An organ and piano reassured us, "This Is My Father's World." A former student of mine, with a voice more mellow than most disc jockeys', did the opening ritual; a bright-eyed, two-year-old boy in a chocolate-colored, vested suit, dangled his feet noiselessly over the edge of the pew. From the minister we heard the age-old story of the prodigal son, but there was nothing old nor dated about the way she told it. I sat mesmerized by her vivid details, felt the exhilaration in the heart of the father as he raced down the dusty road to welcome his wayward son. Without wasting a word, the minister made us see how relevant, how contemporary the story is.

After lunch I returned to the village for a joyous occasion. A couple had lived together and worked together for fifty years — truly a cause for celebration! They had raised five strong sons, most of them builders like their father. One of their wives, so pretty in purple, gave me a welcoming hug at the door and introduced me to her teenage daughter at the guest book. She looked as radiant as a princess in her softly-draped, white dress.

Yellow daisy table arrangements and yellow rose corsages brought a promise of warm spring days inside.

There were uncles, aunts, cousins and friends from close by and far away, and with all of us exclaiming and greeting at once, it wasn't easy to hear — but it was easy to read the happiness on faces. I wouldn't be shocked if the glow on the bride's face was even brighter than fifty years ago!

For one who had avoided spreading germs for two weeks, I had indeed become reckless and inconsiderate.

Later in the afternoon, I joined community residents and visitors for tea at a home tastefully furnished in a pleasant blend of the old and the new. I chose coffee, set my mug on the brick hearth of the handsome fireplace, felt so at home and not at all like Cinderella.

Here there was truly a mixture of personalities and life styles: some commuted daily to work in the city; some made a living locally; some ladies blended careers with motherhood and still managed to set a warm supper on the table by nightfall; some now lived in the same houses their parents had lived in; some had graduated from a degree in parenthood to pursue the marvelous profession of grandparenthood. A young mother of two was in her second year of law school; one visiting lady, active in politics, commented that her spinach had broken through the topsoil despite the late spring; my grandson's community-conscious Little League Coach told me to tell Eric to start getting in shape for the spring season. Here were Methodists, Baptists, Episcopalians, Catholics, and I'm sure, those of other faiths, all coming together to chat, not only about today's headline topics, but about forsythia ready to bloom, apple crop expectations, and family plans for Easter.

On the way home I drove alongside the rustic, stone building that had long been a picturesque landmark in the village, serving through the years as a warehouse, a feed store, and last, a unique brass shop. In late fall the pyracantha bush clinging to the stone front dons its deep scarlet berries and thrills those who live close and those who are passing through. I wouldn't be surprised to know that Civil War bullets ricocheted off the building's fortress-like walls, and I know for sure that it has withstood thunderstorms, high winds, and even yet, the jar and rumble of the daily freight train that runs a few yards behind it.

Tomorrow night, again, I'll turn on the television set and listen to the chilling AIDS statistics, look at the blown-up, glamorized photographs of serial killers on magazine fronts, and gasp at the latest, uncovered scandals in the political campaigns — but tonight, I'll think about organ music and colored glass windows, and I'll remember animated voices and laughter, handshakes and hugs, and people, who out of common concerns, have bonded together, people whose faces and voices say, "We like *where* we are, and we like *who* we are!"

When I do listen to the negative segments in tomorrow night's newscast, thoughts of this day will comfort me. Somehow, I will know that my village, like the old stone building, will be here for a long, long time!

The Village Landmark

What *They* Taught *Me*

The air is cooler this August morning; the western breeze is fresh, shadows are longer, shades are deeper, and the feeling sweeps over me again! I recognize it instantly.

Without warning, on some August morning during each of the twenty-five years I taught young people (and even since I retired), the identical, nostalgic, memory-laden feeling will suddenly surface. The emotion is accented with composition books, construction paper, red marking pens, and there's also a faint trace of the smell of crayon wax (probably left over from my childhood).

Each August, people would ask, "Are you eager for school to start?" Many used the word "anxious" instead of "eager," which was most likely the more appropriate word.

I always replied, "Well, not really," but invariably, I would add, "I am excited about it, though! "

- Time to plan a bulletin board (I never once did one that was truly artistic).
- Time to sort my grammar cartoon posters (Snoopy can glamorize nouns and verbs).
- Time to re-learn the operational techniques of the ditto machine (Yes, I said "ditto." It's a blessing I retired in 1982. The computer system would have

swallowed me whole!).

- And above all else, time to make Lesson Plans!

Looking back, I realize I thoroughly enjoyed the lesson planning; that part of teacher preparation was challenging. Many plans failed later in the classroom, some were moderately successful, and a few (I can easily recall) bordered on being inspirational. For the latter category, I never ceased to be grateful.

Now — today — I ask myself, "What did I teach those young people?" I wait, no answer comes. No lilting, little voice chirps up merrily and says, "Oh, you taught them so much!" And then I know why there is no reply to my silent query. I can't remember what I taught them, but I do remember what they taught me!

Surprisingly, perhaps, I know now that I learned not only from the well-adjusted and the normal and gifted child: from the restless, I learned patience; from the lonely, I learned compassion; from the rebellious, I learned tolerance; from the totally indifferent, I learned to better cope with personal failure.

From all of them over the years I know I gained a keener, more profound knowledge of what life is really all about.

A gray mist covered our farm yesterday. As I drove out the lane in early morning, I followed a procession of five deer silently marching in single file (like a troop of gray-coated soldiers on a reconnaissance mission) down through the rock break. I suddenly remembered a paper that Doug Morris, an eleventh-grader, had laid on my desk one morning. It had not been an assignment. Doug wrote,

> The sunrise was magnificent. The shades of red, orange, and blue mixed to form an inspirational portrait heralding the birth of another day. Through the fluffy, stained clouds, rays of sunlight beamed upon a most wondrous sight five deer vaulted the old gray fence a hundred yards from my window, a buck and four doe in a soaring leap that ripped my heart from my breast. At the same instant, a flock of geese exploded into flight. Soaring, beating, they carried my soul with them, and tears ran down my face. The clouds parted letting the sun illuminate and sear into my mind forever that unforgettable moment. I wept unabashed.

Each day now my life is richer because those young people opened my eyes to the beauty in our world.

No doubt my primary goal in teaching was to accent the importance of character building. I shall never forget the day an advanced English class discussed Emerson's gem of an essay, "Self Reliance." That hour was a teacher's dream come true. Failures can fade into the background if such an hour comes even once in a teacher's career — when all eyes sparkle, when everyone contributes, and when no one rises to leave when the bell sounds. Out of that hour came a short essay by Eric Bates, a senior. I'd like to quote some lines from his paper:

> A better world can be achieved only through Improvement of self. I cannot change the actions of my fellow man; though I may plead, argue, coax, or soil my hands with his blood, I cannot touch his soul unless my own is pure. My own thoughts I control; my own destiny I guide. So, if with every passing day, I can approach perfection of character by even a fraction of an inch, then I have accomplished something. And when I truly believe I am what I should be, then I can approach my brother with outstretched heart and hand and say, 'Come, let us talk of things that were, things that are, and especially, of things that can be!'

When I read the above to that senior class next day, I could see in their faces that they were relieved to know that the quality they were striving for — strength of character — was both tangible and attainable.

But most of all, these young people taught me love. They assured me so many times and in so many touching ways that nothing matters as much. In fact, they convinced me so completely that I borrowed their theory and applied it in working with them.

Consequently, I did not encounter frequent discipline problems — because I used their formula. I cared for them, I told them I cared, and I tried hard to praise them for what they did well before I pointed out to them what they did poorly. Their response left me singing the praises of the power of positive reinforcement.

Over the years they allowed me to be human, they laughed with me when I made mistakes (and I did — often!), and they gently forgave my weaknesses.

They showered me with smiles, kind words, respect, countless tokens, plus standing ovations that left me weak-kneed, teary, and speechless. I can still feel that warmth. Even today, nine years after retiring, contact with these former students is a healing balm for the emotional aches and pains of "growing older."

A broader, deeper concept of love was pointed out to us by a talented and lovely student, Laura. Her works told us that real love does not expect reward or compensation. We must continue to love even if that love isn't returned, acknowledged, or recognized. She enlightened us in a powerful poem entitled "Blessed Is the Fool:"

Blessed is the fool,
He smiles through tears of others' pain,
Nurses broken hearts to strength again.
Marches on to battles of ridicule that never will be won -
Blessed is the fool!

He climbs the sunbeams of others' dreams,
Gathers rainbow colors for others to enjoy,
Loving things that will love him never
Blessed is the fool!

He fears not loneliness, the crowds are his foe,
He walks alone down every tear swept path,
Giving smiles to others' cries,
Making all things right,
Blessed is the fool!

Recently, many have cautioned me ("cushioned" would be a better word), "Dess, things are different now. You should be glad you retired when you did."

I realize there are ominous, destructive forces threatening not only our youth, but every generation; I know priorities are dangling precariously on undesirable fringes of today's society. However, when a close teacher friend was my luncheon guest Sunday, I asked her if she was eager to return to school. Her reply, like mine years before, was, "I hate to see summer end. But there's always excitement about going back."

I asked the eleventh-grade son of a friend the same question, expecting to hear "Mercy, no!"

I heard "No, I'm never ready to go back, but I still get excited when it's close."

I've long been convinced that the most essential element in the learning process is enthusiasm; could it be that so long as lengthening shadows and deeper shades of an August day spark excitement, in teachers and in those whom they teach (administrators, too!), our future is in capable hands?

Last week I overheard a conversation in a local fast food restaurant. I didn't intentionally eavesdrop, but an attractive lady in her mid-thirties announced to her two companions, "Honestly, the young people today are worthless. Most of them have no morals, no intelligence, no ambition!" I didn't ask her to please substitute the word "Some" for "Most;" I didn't suggest that she decrease the number of derogatory generalizations about our young people. I just sat there — smiling, quiet, and a trifle smug — and I thought to myself,

"You are missing so much. I know. I've seen the stars in their eyes!"

The Secret of the Sealed Attic Door

The ivy that envelops the entire north end of our four-story, Georgian, brick house has been a constant source of comment.

Many have said, "It's so rustic, so picturesque, so English."

Others have warned, "Dess, you'd better get that stuff off your old house; it'll pull every bit of the mortar out of the bricks."

Then one day a friend (?) grinned and said, "Some warm, fall day a big black snake will climb up that vine, slither under the eaves, and spend the winter in your attic!"

Last September I decided to go up to the attic and search for the shoebox full of Jim's love letters to me. My letters to him were hidden in a downstairs closet, but I could not locate his to me. The situation made me a bit uneasy. I would hesitate to give his letters an "X" rating (after all, they were written in 1947 and 1948), but I would label a few of them somewhere between "R" and "PG."

Jauntily, I climbed the four flights of steps, ducked my head to clear the low attic door frame, opened the door, and stood frozen. The spacious room, with a window on each side of the chimney, was light on such a sunny day — too light!

The prophecy had come true! There he lay. Please, may I use the pronoun "he", for had it been a "she", there could have already been prospective offspring?

There, sunning in luxurious comfort, lay a black snake, casually coiled, lengthy, and wide in circumference. I didn't utter a sound; I couldn't. Softly — very softly — I closed the door and raced down the steps to call my son. How he ever understood what I said I don't know, but evidently he heard the phrase "snake in the attic."

He had heard me relate how I, as a little girl growing up in the hills, had so often been warned (and rightfully so!) when I went out to play on the rocks along the creek bank or walk down the railroad to Mamaw's house, "Dessie, be careful about the copperheads!" I was well aware that the snake sunning in the attic was not a copperhead, but my emotions had never allowed differentiation.

The following five to seven minutes were among the longest in my life. I prayed, "Please, God, don't let him move. Don't let him hide under an old rug or crawl back under the eaves. He and I cannot live together in this house; I don't care if he does plan to hole up and remain immobile all winter. I really don't want him dead. It's fine with me if Nick lets him loose in the limestone ledge or puts him up in the hay loft but please not in my attic or under my bed!"

I was in the downstairs hall to welcome (an understatement) Nick and his seven-year-old son. I still don't know why it was Eric carrying the pitchfork instead of Nick. No farm implement serves better to pick up and drape a serpent than a pitchfork. I could hear Nick saying, "Buddy, be careful with that pitchfork. You'll break something." I wouldn't have said a word if he had demolished the most priceless antique in the house!

Down in the hall, I kept repeating, "Please still be there." Several moments of silence — then Eric called out, "We're bringing it down, Grandma. Go over in the living room so you won't have to see it. He hangs way down." I wished he hadn't said that!

I never did ask Nick whether he deposited him in the barn or in the rock ledge. I hope it was the ledge; there are plenty of holes for him to crawl into for the winter, and the ledge is a longer distance from the house then the barn is. In the future, one of Mr. Snake's grandchildren might inherit his adventurous spirit.

Considering the fact that labor would be cheaper than my funeral expenses, the next day Nick had a friend do surgery on the ivy. An entire construction crew with heavy duty equipment could not have severed the ivy tendrils from the bricks, so Eddie and his men cut a swath — inch-by-inch, foot-by-foot, eight feet wide, halfway up the end of the house, hoping to discourage future climbers.

Another worker sealed the attic door with heavy plastic, reinforcing the bottom. If, by some calamitous chance, a relative of my displaced friend did get into the attic, he couldn't get out the door to embark on an exploratory expedition.

I doubt that I'll ever remove the plastic!

Years from now, on a warm, rainy afternoon, one of my browsing descendants who is sentimental about times past might sit by the window where the snake lay and smile wistfully over the letters Jim wrote to me.

By then, society might have promoted them to a "G" rating — or even created a new category — "B" — for Beautiful!

Somebody Is Home

At 7:30 this morning, with one small, common, everyday object, I did something that will change my lifestyle for the next seven or eight months.

During these months, I'll probably need to take a bath, not only before I go to bed, but every time I entertain guests or leave the farm. I will make more trips to the beauty shop. I will do additional laundry. I'll buy stronger liquid cleaner. I'll replace my skinny, string mop.

My shoulder muscles will feel sore, and my usually supple knees will stiffen because I will constantly be scrambling about for scattered fragments like an experienced bag lady.

Probably I'll need to replenish my supply of poison ivy medication.

Every time heavy rain clouds form or snow begins to fall, I will rush frantically out the kitchen door.

Mentally, I will have to remain more alert all day and far into the night.

No doubt you've already guessed what I did this morning that will change my life so drastically.

With a single match, after I noticed the forty-degree reading on the outdoor thermometer, I started the fire in the kitchen wood stove.

I did this after removing the ashes I should have scooped out months ago. Then, bundling up in robe, sweater, knee socks and durable gloves, I went outside to last year's meager wood pile, picked up, piece by piece, bark, sticks, board slivers and stuffed them in a brown paper bag. I then leaned the crippled wheelbarrow against the fence for support and loaded it with round, locust logs, wheeled it up to the kitchen porch steps and propped it up again.

I tried to forget that my porch linoleum had just been waxed; I did put an old, plastic tablecloth under the stack of wood, but everybody knows the "offal" from a pile of fire wood can seep through a sheet of metal.

True, it had been a tiring morning workout, but I was ready to go. The flames burned high and steadily.

If your house doesn't have some rooms with thirteen-foot ceilings, and if your annual heating bill is less than two thousand dollars you may not understand the rashness of some of my predictions.

I'm sure you understand the increase in cleaning chores; if you've ever once taken out ashes, you know the particles possess strange aeronautical powers. They float leisurely in the air until you have finished wiping all counter and table tops and then calmly settle.

You know that poison ivy often looks dead but isn't. You no doubt realize that as soon as the sky clouds over with either rain, snow, or sleet, I'll rush outside to see if the big plastic sheet is sufficiently secured over my pile of wood. It never is.

Now why do I need to improve my mental prowess, my perception? The answer is simple. Two times in four years I have opened the stove's bottom draft door to speed up the heating process, wandered off to do something important, caught the chimney on fire, and nearly burned down the house. The local fire departments might not appreciate being summoned to Shenstone Farm a third time, and I cannot blame them.

You might ask, "Is it worth it? The sore muscles, the dirt?" Is it worth it? Yes! There's a certain by-product of wood-heater heat that mysteriously envelops us with a tingling sense of well being, a "cared-for" feeling not found in any other fuel.

As I lingered over my morning coffee, I thought, "A wood heater performs a dual role: it warms the body and the heart."

And don't you agree that smoke rolling out of a chimney seems to send a signal to a cold, outside world that somebody is home?

Not the Panoramas

During my recent visit to Kentucky, my two sisters and my niece took me to the Smokies for a long weekend to celebrate my milestone birthday.

When we drove up the mountain road and stopped at the rustic gatehouse to pick up our lodging reservations, the receptionist said, "The decor in this townhouse is beautiful, but I'm afraid you'll be disappointed in the view. There's no panorama so common in the Smokies. You can't see far."

The exterior of the unit was impressive and majestic French chateau architecture, softened with touches of wood.

The lady at the gatehouse was right about the decor and the facilities. The kitchen was complete, all conveniences full-sized and spotless; the dining area was inviting; a sunken living room promised charm and comfort. Upstairs were two huge bedrooms with king-size beds, plus an enormous hot tub surrounded by stone and mirrors, all rooms tastefully coordinated with lush, jade green carpet, mauve and green accessories, and a variety of wallpaper patterns in dainty sprigs and flowers.

We were so enchanted by the interior that we hesitated (remembering, I'm sure, what the receptionist had told us about the view) to walk out on either of the three balconies.

We plugged in the coffee maker, argued over who would occupy the room with the hot tub, tested the intercom, and admired the octagon-shaped, stained-glass window in one of the bathrooms. Then one sister walked out on the upstairs balcony; I remember hearing her exclaim, "How could anyone say this is not a good view?" Sure, there was no panorama, no layer of misty mountains in the distance, no river meandering among the rocks — but there was a view!

From the balcony, we could almost touch the trees: the sugar maples, gum, cedars, sycamores, tall, slender birches. Crisp, frosty mornings had stripped them of most of their leaves, but many, though brown, still clung, reluctant to give way to winter. A bluebird darted sassily from one branch to another. The breeze moved the branches slightly, making a sighing, soothing sound.

Later, the crock pot, full of simmered beef roast, smelled divine, and the same sister who cooked had thought to bring tall, tapered candles that melted into multi-colored wax sculptures; one finished product looked like a flamingo.

By far, the outstanding feature of the living room was the fireplace with its enormous, raised, stone hearth that wrapped all around the front and into the corner of the room. Flames fed warmth about us and reflected in the ceiling-length glass windows.

As night closed in, the wind rose, and the tree limbs brushed close to the balcony. I had never before realized that wind in dry, November leaves sounds like falling sleet. The weather report predicted a record low, but it was warm inside.

The warmth came not only from the flames and embers of the fireplace, it came from the small talk, the laughter, the togetherness, the caring, the memories of times past, and the plans for tomorrow — all woven into swatches of time that could make one feel young forever!

When compared to the pleasures above, all the extras; the hot tub, waterbeds, dimmer light switches, automatic timers, intercom system; paled into insignificance.

And I thought, "In life, it's not the panoramas that count, not the wide sweeps, not the overlooks, not the vistas.

We don't need to see far when there is so much up close!"

High Energy Level — Asset or Liability?

For years I wailed, "Oh, if I just had more energy, I could move mountains!" Then suddenly a few months ago, I realized I did have more energy! I couldn't quite move mountains, but I managed to relocate a few hills.

However, lately I've learned that a high energy level can produce a severe side effect. This would not occur in normal people who perform with moderation, who properly pace themselves, who don't undertake three times as much as anyone nearing a seventh decade should.

During these high-level energy months, my body had held up well, but last week I noticed the warning symptoms of a high-energy side effect.

Ten months ago, I promised a lovely lady in Charles Town that I would do a program for her Church Circle on September 30. Yes, I put it on my calendar. A few days before time, she checked with me. Yes, I'd be there, and I was flattered that she had invited out-of-town guests. Over the weekend, I did a trial run so I'd know exactly where she lived and where to park.

On Monday, a day early (or so I thought), I worked hard on the program, decided what to wear, entertained company that morning, then breezed leisurely into Charles Town that afternoon.

After I got home, the phone rang: "Dess, what's wrong?" my friend whispered. "Are you sick? Were you in a wreck? We went ahead with the business first and waited and waited!" I was horrified and embarrassed beyond words. My quirky mind had rearranged the calendar and made Tuesday, not Monday, the Thirtieth.

The hostess was both kind and courageous. She asked if I would do the program at her house next September and she would call me that morning. She is one brave woman.

The climax, the rude awakening, occurred Wednesday. As the attendant filled my gas tank, she said, "Mrs. Snyder, I hate to tell you, but your inspection sticker has expired."

This couldn't be! I protested, "I know it was done in October last year." "No," she replied gently as I squinted at the sticker, "it was way before that." I can't quote in what month it had been inspected last year for fear of legal incrimination.

This was too much! I had been beset by a new ailment. Monday had become Tuesday and I can't say what month had become October. I hadn't actually forgotten anything; I had simply readjusted the entire time sequence. My high energy level had brought on a severe disorder, a chronic case of Cluttered Mind Syndrome!

What to do about it?

Thursday morning I canceled two outside activities. I spent my time doing little things that couldn't possibly clutter my mind. The syndrome might not disappear immediately, but at least it wouldn't get any worse.

I made Jello by stirring in ice cubes slowly — very slowly. I tackled other uncluttering tasks: Untangled the cords on my three electric blankets; replaced the bag on the upright vacuum cleaner; scrubbed the tree sap spots off the hood of the car; balanced my checkbook ($9.79 off, more accurate than anytime this year), oiled the contrary, one-hundred-ninety-year-old lock on the front door, fully aware that if I used the whole can of oil, I'd still have to give the door a vigorous hip push to lock it.

No longer do I need to worry about my case of cluttered-mind syndrome. The next morning, my energy level was back down to where it used to be.

On Top of, Not Over, the Hill

An observation from my six-year-old granddaughter cushioned the realty of my reaching the age of seventy not long ago. With her dreamy, brown eyes, Martha stared at me across the breakfast table and calmly announced, "You know, Grandma, God made you look kinda funny, and He made you look kinda old, but He didn't make you act old!" For the revelation, I gave her a hug.

On the evening of my eventful birthday, a friend called and inquired, "Well, Old Lady, do you feel like you're over the hill?" Quickly, I replied, "Nope, I feel like I'm on top of, not over, the hill!"

Mentioning the top of the hill brought back memories of a childhood experience. One bright, spring Sunday afternoon when I was six my dad asked what I would like to do for the remainder of the day. Our house was nestled close to a tall mountain; rugged, steep and heavily wooded. Already, in early April, I had journeyed around the logging road to see the field of delicate, wild iris; the family had taken a picnic lunch of Kool-aid and cream-filled, waffle cookies back to the big rock halfway up the hill; everyday after school I had gathered the eggs from the overturned washtub nest beside the mountain stream. All these things I had done, so I think Daddy was surprised when I asked him, "Could you take me all the way to the top of the hill? I'd like to see what's on the other side."

In mid-afternoon we set out on our climb. More than once he had to tell me, "Slow down, Dessie. If you go too fast, you'll tire out too quickly." Periodically he would caution, "Let me go in front. It's warm today, and a copperhead might be out sunning himself." Halfway up the hill we stopped to rest on the rocks and to drink from the sparkling stream. If the brambles were too tangled or the blackberry vines too thick, he picked me up in his arms and carried me.

At last, there we were on top! Oh, I was so excited! I could see so much! After all, I had never been more than twenty-five miles away from home, into the county seat. I really couldn't, but it seemed I could see almost that far now! All behind me was familiar, the prosperous mining camp with the duplex houses, the tipple, my school, the huge company store, our frame house beside the creek, Papaw Stanley's two-story farm house, the country road. I don't know what I expected to find on the other side of the hill, but what I did see was in no way spectacular.

In the valley below me sat an L-shaped log house, probably three rooms, with smoke curling from a chimney. The day was warm, but the kitchen cookstove had to be fired even on Sunday. Enclosed in a split rail fence lot was a Jersey cow; surprisingly I could clearly hear the tinkle of her bell sounding a background melody. All Kentucky mountain cows wore bells in the springtime. The vegetation was so lush they would not voluntarily come in to be milked; they had to be "gone for."

No, the view was not spectacular. Why it appealed to a six-year-old, I do not know, but I remember I stood and looked a long time. It was so hushed, so peaceful. My young mind could not have explained it then, but I know now that what I felt after reaching the top of that mountain and what I saw in the valley below gave me a "sense of well-being" that I had never known before.

That same feeling (I could even hear the tinkle of the cowbell) came the day I reached seventy. I was on top, not over, the hill! And I knew why I was on top, because of the People in my life!

- A father who not only took me to the top of the mountain when I was a child, but who made me a pine dressing table and shipped it 200 miles by railway express so that my college dormitory room would look more cheerful.
- A mother who sacrificed the fund she had set aside for new drapes to buy me a rather risque negligee and gown outfit when I got married.
- Two sisters who were always (and still are) my "buddies." A few days ago they took me back to the "hills of home" to see the mountain I had climbed as a child. I did not attempt a reenactment!

Even before Jim and I were married, I used to take a jug of iced tea to him out in the hay field on hot, July afternoons and he would smile and say, "You didn't have to do that." So many times in the forty years of our special marriage, I heard him say those same words. He gave so much and demanded so little. I'm glad that one night not long before he left us, when the song "You Are the Wind Beneath My Wings" was sung on television, I said to him, "That's what you've been to me!" Had it not been for him, I'm sure I could not today boast, "I am on top of, not over, the hill!"

Someone said, "The greatest day in the life of parents is when they realize their children are standing on their own two feet!" My two seem to be doing more than that. There seems to be a very comfortable (for me) borderline role reversal. I'm sure they mutter, "What kind of mess has Odessa gotten herself into now?" but they respect me enough to let me stand by myself. I know fully well, that they and the caring partners they married are always close by to steady me when I stumble.

The term "in-law" does not fit those in my family designated as such. The bonding I share with them is too warm for a phrase with legal terminology.

— And grandchildren! I know it was their touch, their laughter, that kept me from going over the hill during some trying times of the past few years. The eleven-year-old granddaughter gave me a lift last week. When the eighth-grade grandson informed me he had not received a zero in homework for a long time, I pretended to faint, fell on the dining room floor. When I rose, Natalie quipped, "Grandma you're the only old woman I know who can get down on the floor and get up all by herself!"

Often, friends are referred to as the "extras" in our lives. Extras can be dispensed with. My friends are the bright red and yellow leaves that cling to branches in mid-November; they are the rays of sunlight that part a heavy cloud and give promise of a bright tomorrow.

Over the years the young people I taught kept me climbing; they still do. Just yesterday I ran into a handsome man who stared at me a moment then exclaimed, "Why , Mrs. Snyder, I haven't seen you since you taught me in 1961!" I was thrilled that he even recognized me after thirty years!

Then there's my community — for forty-five years they have reached out to me in a thousand wonderful ways. The poet said, "Home is where the heart is." My heart is here!

Family, friends, community — they've been there all along playing the role of my dad the day we reached the top of the hill — cautioning me now and then to slow down, carrying me over the true danger spots. I could never have made it alone.

You might ask, "Will you go over the hill — ever?" Perhaps, but I know that these incredible people will take my hand and gently lead me down.

It could be that in the distance, I'll once again hear the soothing tinkle of a cowbell!

My Little Green-backed Reader

This winter I have an enormous task ahead of me. I must sort my books. They are everywhere — under beds, in dish cupboards, in boxes on the attic stairs, some actually in bookcases. A Perry Mason paperback mystery rests on top of the *Complete Anthology of Shakespeare* given to me by a student when I retired from teaching. If a friend asked to borrow *Gone With The Wind*, or if my son needed his college algebra textbook, I would be a week finding them.

So many books — and yet one is missing! I am so sorry I did not keep my *Primer* (pronounced "Primmer"). Many have never heard the term used educationally, certainly not with that particular pronunciation.

In my Kentucky graded school system, when students graduated from the eighth grade, actually they had completed nine full years of schooling. First, we went to an all-day primer. The setup was similar to today's kindergarten, but the pupils did not enter until the age of six. I had learned to read, more or less accidentally, from salt, sugar and rice boxes, so I stayed in the primer only a semester, but I never forgot my little green-backed reader.

So many lessons in living we learned from that reader! We learned from Robert Louis Stevenson to relax by going up in a swing — "up in the air so blue." We learned to accomplish difficult tasks little by little from the thirsty crow that painstakingly dropped enough pebbles into a tall pitcher in order to raise the water level high enough for him to drink. We learned that it's ridiculous to be afraid all the time, to expect the worst to happen, from the actions of the "Three Sillies." The fate of "The Little Boy Who Cried Wolf" has alerted many generations.

The last selection in my little green book was written by Eugene Field of "Little Boy Blue" fame. I truthfully didn't understand it then — the underlying philosophy was a bit profound for a six-year-old, but I think I understand it now. Perhaps you will recall it. The title was "Contentment."

In life, all of us have to learn that quite often contentment and acceptance are synonymous. We cannot be truly happy in this complicated world until we realize there are some situations we simply cannot "fix." Many things we can and should change. When I'm exhausted from trying to alter a facet of my life (so frustrating, I'll admit!), when I am finally convinced that my only sensible alternative is to try to adjust to the situation, I think of Field's little poem in the back of my *Primer*. I'd like to paraphrase it for you.

> One spring a little, red hen hatched out her babies, but there was a slight inconsistency. There were four

chicks and six ducks. Did that bother her? Almost proudly, she shrugged her wings and said, "'Tis very rare that hens have baby ducks as well as chicks."

Next hatching time — all chicks, no ducks. Not a mite ruffled, the mother said, "My babies now will stay ashore and consequently cannot drown."

But next season, believe it or not, they were all ducks. Did she panic? Calmly, she declared, "A little water now and then will certainly do us all some good."

But woe was she! Next spring there were no babies at all! Guess what she said — "'Tis best these things are so, for babies are a dreadful care!"

The poet summarizes by stating that we could learn a lesson from the little, red hen:

She ne'er presumed to take offence
At any fate that might befall,
But meekly bowed to Providence;
She was contented, that was all.

I do not believe Providence always expects us to meekly bow. There are many things we can and must change, but we surely can take some tips from Mrs. Red Hen.

The closing analogy may seem strange coming from someone who can't swim a stroke — me!

When the tides ride high in our lives, we have three choices. Often, if we are about to go under, we can fight; we can battle the waves. If we can't fight, we can return to shore. If we can't do either, we had better learn to float.

A few times in my life, when the waves engulfed me, I've been a powerful fighter. Also, I'm an experienced escapist; many times I've returned to shore — but I do wish I could learn to be a better "floater"!

You see, I don't always practice what I preach.

"Reading, Writing, and 'Rithmatic"
in West Virginia.

Handicaps Can Have Compensations

Not long ago my sister-in-law and I were discussing physical handicaps and the different ways people deal with them. Suddenly, she added, "Your handicap hasn't bothered you all that much, has it?" For a moment, I did a double take. Handicap? What handicap? Then, of course, I knew. I did have a handicap, a minor one compared with the afflictions of others, but still a handicap.

I entered the world with only two percent vision in the corner of the left eye and nystagmus (involuntary motion that prevents proper focusing) in the right "good" eye. Between the bridge of the nose and the far corner of the left eye, there is no vision.

Problems resulted early. The weak muscles in the left eye pulled inward, producing the condition graphically referred to as "cross-eyed." I don't recall being painfully self-conscious about the deformity when I was very young. Children are resilient. I was busy sitting on rocks along the creek bank and roaming the hills. Now, though, I can remember that sometimes people didn't look directly at me when they talked to me; I'm sure the irregularity made them uncomfortable, and too, they didn't want to embarrass me.

Compensations began. My close-up vision was good enough for me to learn to read even before I started to school — and how I enjoyed that! Mother, Daddy and my baby sister made a wonderful audience.

However, in second grade, near-sightedness began in the "good" eye. It was soon so extreme that I would have to rise out of my front row seat and walk all the way to the blackboard to copy spelling words or a math problem. The path to the blackboard, I know now, was long and humiliating, but not because of the teacher or my classmates. Miss Blanton, my beautiful, auburn-haired teacher, was my support. With gentle words and encouraging smiles, she did much, not only to help me make that solo journey to the blackboard, but also to help me face the years ahead. She died the following year with tuberculosis, leaving me puzzled and devastated, but her positive influence is with me yet today.

Looking back, I know that most of my classmates were considerate, too. We speak often of how children can be innocently cruel to those who are different. They teased me about my red hair but not about my crossed eye. In fact, my elementary years were quite normal. My girl friends and I giggled, read the Little Colonel series of books, held sleep-overs, and sometimes fussed. Once, three of us had a "falling out" in sixth grade — didn't talk for three days — because Gladys polished my nails with flamingo pink nail polish and didn't do Charlene's. In eighth grade a very serious, scholarly boy was quite attentive to me. I really don't remember wondering, "How could he have a crush on me when I'm cross-eyed?" My heart just didn't skip beats when he was around, even when he gave me a pair of lacy, blue, satin garters for Christmas!

What I'm saying is that even though I was somewhat maimed physically and cosmetically in those early years, I did not feel ostracized. I know I tried hard to achieve academically, but I don't think I was competitive with others. I had to prove to myself that I could achieve.

No doubt it was psychologically significant that during the summer following eighth-grade graduation, I got out Mother's picture box and cut myself out of all the photographs (from the neck up). I tried to convince myself that a camera tended to emphasize the crossed eye.

Even in Biblical times, the age of twelve was a milestone in life. It was for me.

For years the optometrists had attempted to fit me with glasses that would improve vision in the good eye. No lens helped, so I had never worn glasses. Nothing, not even surgery, could change the left eye. Finally, a concerned and skilled doctor in a nearby West Virginia coal town said he believed he could fit me with lens that would lessen the nearsightedness and thereby improve my distance vision.

Having received some double promotions in grade school, I entered ninth grade when I was eleven years old. On October 20, my twelfth birthday, my whole life was transformed; a world with more light and color than I had ever seen opened before me. On that day I went to get my first pair of glasses. Daddy took off work on the railroad, picked me up at school in his Model A Ford, and took me into town. I remember so well, wearing my new glasses, riding alongside the river on the way home. I glanced up — the hills were covered with flames of color, leaves brilliant. I could see them, each tiny patch of russet, crimson, gold, even individual leaves. All my life a mountain had been a blur, one tree indistinguishable from the other, form flowing into form, nothing distinct. Along the top of the hill, trees had shed their leaves early. For the first time I saw bare tree limbs fringed symmetrically against the bright, blue October sky, and suddenly, I was crying. Tears poured down my face. Daddy handed me his navy bandanna, and so concerned, asked, "Dessie, what's wrong? Are you sick?" and softly I replied, "No, Daddy, I can see!"

The four high school years were exciting and meaningful. At graduation I cried as if my life was over, not beginning. Could it be that during the years, my eye muscles had straightened? It did seem that when I looked at myself in the mirror, I didn't notice it as much. Anyway, in my senior pictures, I made sure I turned my head to the left so the crossed eye would turn outward, not in, and appear more normal.

Strange as it may seem, the two deepest emotional cuts came during college — from adults.

By then, I was so sure my abnormal eye was less noticeable. One day in junior college our professor passed out our literature exams. Behind me sat my secret crush — a tall, black-haired basketball player. When the teacher announced "Odessa made ninety-six, the highest score," my hero whispered to a pal across from him, "No wonder. She can read both pages at the same time." I felt numb and betrayed.

Then, believe it or not, the worst hurt came in senior college from a professional. By then, I was convinced that not many were even aware of the problem anymore. We girls, clad only in angel robes, were in line for our physicals. The doctor was friendly, but his voice was gruff and a bit intimidating. I stood, nervous, and I'm sure, hopeful that he would miraculously overlook the visual weakness. I should have been more realistic. He said, "Now, let's see if you have an eye problem", and then (and I know fully well he had no intention of embarrassing me), in a voice loud enough for the whole room to hear, — "You surely do have an eye problem. You're cross-eyed!" My world crumbled, not because he recognized the defect (after all, he was a physician), but because he had announced it to my peers when I had hoped they didn't know.

However, I rationalized later, "I do believe he didn't notice it right away, and he's a doctor!"

Year after year the same prescription for nearsightedness sufficed. Reading bedtime stories to my two children was a pleasure. Teaching caused no severe strain. In fact, a real emotional breakthrough came when I resumed teaching after my children were older. In an English class, we were discussing a short story about a blind woman. I told them about my problem, explaining that compared to other people's handicaps, mine was minor; a boy's hand went up. My eleventh grader asked a question I'll never forget, "Which eye *was* it, Mrs. Snyder?"

More and more I had come to realize that along with the handicap, there had come compensations; some came from the kindness in the hearts of others, some from increased medical knowledge, and some from my own maturity.

Ten years ago glaucoma began in the good eye; that same year the FDA released a new eye drop that until this day has kept my pressure under control and the glaucoma in remission.

When a cataract formed over the good eye four years ago, I found again what it had been like before glasses were fitted in ninth grade. Vision became hazy; trees mingled into an indistinct blur; reading was a chore; my favorite television programs were no longer enjoyable. Then, when the proper time came, my wonderfully kind and skilled ophthalmologist implanted a new lens, and two days later, feeling quite mod in my glamorous sunglasses, I began to resume an almost normal routine.

Also, an unexpected compensation manifested itself immediately following the surgery. I was amazed by how much help the two percent vision in the corner of the left eye could be. Of course while the patch was on, I had to dispense with my makeup, but I didn't one time bump into the coffee table, and I could tell that my granddaughter was wearing a blue sweatshirt!

I guess I always knew the faulty focusing condition in the good eye would eventually interfere more. The only major problem the nystagmus had previously caused was preventing me from driving at night. Just this year, reading after darkness sets in has become a strain. The good eye hurts when I look at television too long. My same dear doctor who did the lens implant told me gently, "You know, that eye has borne the burden of two eyes for a long, long time." I grinned and teased him, "Are you insinuating I'm not young any more?" He laughed and explained, "The eye is tired. It's straining and protesting now."

Often now at night the good eye is difficult to focus (seldom in daytime — a great compensation!). I can give up reading at night if during the daytime, I can see the new, green shoots on the maple tree in the front yard, the lilac bush blooming in early May, the squirrel flitting about on the board fence, a rainbow over the barn field, or a grandchild walking down the road for an after school visit. Right now, even on a cloudy day, I can clearly read road signs. I can write with ease on lined paper. I can hint for a VCR for my birthday, tape my night television programs, and spend leisurely, winter afternoons watching them. When night comes, I can play my stereo, call a friend, and count my blessings.

I am aware of the fact that the eye that has worked so diligently for seventy years could some day just cease to function. There's even a compensation when I realize that — a point of light, so to speak! I honestly believe I could learn to take care of myself with the infinitesimal two percent vision in the corner of the left eye. That tiny portion of my sight remains undamaged, and, I like to think, ready for emergency use.

One might say, "Two percent isn't much."

Even the tiniest of candles sends out a tremendous amount of light compared to total darkness!

What I Want — to Give — for Christmas

I did the final draft of my 1991 Christmas shopping list early this morning, sitting at my desk in front of the southeast window, watching the sun spread over the fields, and sipping a second cup of coffee.

At the time, the task seemed quite simple — a jumble of jewelry, bed linens, tools, sweat shirts, cassettes, Nintendo games, doll clothes, underwear, dusters with matching scuffs, and homemade candy.

The first time I read the completed list, I felt it was quite satisfactory. I had left out no one; surely the items were what they needed or wanted or both. I read the list again, and the thought came to me, "Seems you've made this list before. Repetitious, isn't it? Didn't you give some of the same people the same articles one or two or three years ago?" Actually, on closer scrutiny, some items seemed a bit ordinary, even unexciting, but with limited finances and, I'll admit, possibly limited imagination and creative abilities, what can one give?

I put down my pen, took the last sip of coffee, and thought, "Suppose, just suppose, my means, my imagination, and my generosity were unlimited, what would I give?" The revised list bore no resemblance to the first.

To my loved ones who are already or soon will be on Medicare (my age bracket), regardless of gender, I would give gilt-bordered achievement plaques, praising them for proving by their lifestyles, that living in the later years can be meaningful and full, that the enchantment is still there.

Dreams are difficult to package. So often they are wispy and ethereal. But dreams I would give to my young friends, not a facsimile of mine or someone else's dream, but their own to climb toward and to hold on to. Subtly, I would suggest to them that when they reached a goal, they would pause long enough on the plateau to shout, "I did it!" Stopping long enough to realize they are content with their world and with themselves will fortify them to press on to the next goal.

So many close to me (most of them younger, I'll admit) have such hectic schedules. They are caught up in the frenzy of a too-demanding career, constantly plagued by the modern malady of epidemic proportions called "making ends meet." I, too, am not immune to that malady. They are innocent victims of the "not enough" syndrome — not enough dollars in the paycheck, not enough hours in the day, not enough time for the family, but perhaps, worst of all, not enough time for themselves. Their rigid routines simply do not allow for the recouping of depleted resources. Considering their dilemma, I would rate their present day performances miraculous, but how I'd love to lift a sizable slot of hours out of each week, wrap it, and label it "Yours Alone!"

A fringe benefit that was not cancelled when I retired from the field of education was the relationships with my teacher friends. To each of them, I would give a microscopic, video camera that would project into the future and produce instant flashbacks. On camera, one teacher friend might watch a scientist explaining in detail his newly discovered cure for cancer, and the teacher might say, "He was my dreamer, but I just let him dream!" Another teacher, on the video screen, would see the boy who used to pump gas at the local filling station. He had just designed the sensational new American-made sports car. My friend would comment, "He never did hand his homework in on time, but he could fix anything!" When the screen showed an attractive lady in a cozy kitchen, busy mixing a chocolate cake from "scratch," another friend might say, "Somehow I knew when I had her in English class that her qualities could someday help prevent the dissolution of the American family."

Right now some close to me are facing momentous decisions, desiring change, but not sure which road to take, asking "Am I headed in the right direction? Is this step in my life too drastic? Will I find this path so dark and difficult I'll have to turn back?" To them I would give a magic candle, the kind used to enchant children at birthday parties. When they are blown out, no matter how forceful the puff, they flame up again seconds later and continue to give a light just as bright as before. On the candle base, I would inscribe a simple message, "You'll make it; your strength is like the flame that cannot be extinguished."

During the past year, some dear to me have lost loved ones. For them, I would wrap a cardboard star in silver tinsel to remind them that even in the darkest stage of grief, there is a higher power watching over us. The night sky can be black for a long time, but in our hearts we know that sometime soon the cloud cover will move on out, and there, above us, will be our star.

Rejection has come this year to some close to me. I would give them healing balm to soothe the hurt that always comes when ones they trusted left them lonely and afraid.

To the children of broken homes I know, I would give gaily-colored security blankets, guaranteed to cover their confusion and to make them feel safe and wanted through all their growing years.

I am not licensed to dispense medication, but to those, young or old, who suffer physical or emotional pain — and there are many — I would give hope. Certainly, hope does not package easily. It would not need to be wrapped! Perhaps I could write a note on paper sprayed with the scent of cedar or take a slice of fruit cake when I went to visit. It's the little things that keep us clinging to tomorrow.

Possibly, the gifts I'd like to wrap for my immediate family would be a bit more individualistic.

I would give my son a formula for the reduction of physical and financial uncertainties that can come from the operation of a fourth generation, family dairy farm. The formula would not need to be foolproof, for he loves the land and will work hard to keep it.

To my daughter, I would give the unfaltering assurance that even though hers is an interracial marriage, her two beautiful children will never feel the backlash of bigotry or the sting of intolerance.

For my five grandchildren, I would wrap a box of value symbols to impress upon them what will matter most in their lives ahead: a miniature seashell to remind them to walk softly and see the beauty this world offers; a toy spade to convey to them that hard work is effective therapy; a gold chain to show them how love can link a whole world together; and a stained glass rainbow of faith to prove to them that storms do not last forever.

My shopping list would be finished, all names on the list checked.

I would not enclose a card with my name when I wrapped the gifts. They wouldn't even need to know who the giver was. But I would need an envelope, a red one, I think. Then, for all those loved ones, I would lift the sparkle from the eyes of a baby girl I know, put with it a chunk of curiosity from a baby boy I know, let the red envelope suggest laughter, and seal it with a stamp of love!

I just might do an extra red envelope and keep it for myself.

Everybody comes through the back hall door — not just at Christmas.

"On Christmas Day in the Morning"

Many times during the Christmas seasons since Jim, my husband, passed away, concerned friends and family have asked, "What are your plans for Christmas morning?" Most of them know that my daughter directs Santa Claus to come to their home in Alabama and my son's family welcomes him in their old farmhouse up on the hill. So when the question is asked, I always answer, "I'll be home." Invariably, the query comes, "By yourself?" I can tell by the tone of their voices that the idea startles and bothers them.

In fact, just yesterday a grandson suggested that I drive up to their house; I could just go up over the fields, wouldn't even have to drive out on the road, could just come in my robe and knee socks, and watch them open their presents on Christmas morning. I told him I truly appreciated his sweet invitation, but I preferred coming later in the day, after they had already begun to eat their turkey with the trimmings (even marshmallow-topped sweet potatoes and sauerkraut) dinner. My strict, medical diet prohibits even a sample of the festive food, so it would be far less painful for me to confront a partially consumed bird than to drool over one that was still brown, crusty and intact.

How can I explain to the ones I care about, and who care about me, why being home by myself on Christmas morning will not upset me?

Christmas is not a morning; it's not even totally categorized by Dickens' "Past, Present or To Come." Christmas is cumulative. So much of the magic is in the anticipation, the planning, yes, even in the frustrations and deadlines; the magic lies in the fluttering moments, perhaps some tinged with sadness, some colored with tender overtones, some flavored with laughter.

For me, the Christmas season opens when I first hear the simple carol "Silent Night," but I also felt Christmas last week when the granddaughter and friends danced the "Charleston" in a "Jingle Bells Through the Years" number in her sixth-grade chorus concert.

Later, when my grandson's junior high chorus combined with the band for a spine-tingling finale of familiar carols, ending with a glorious rendition of "Hark, the Herald Angels Sing," I knew Christmas had come.

I desperately needed the thrilling finale to alleviate the embarrassment I had subjected my family and myself to before the program. During my teaching career, every time we were called to the gymnasium, I never ventured above the bottom bleacher. My coordination simply would not permit it. I honestly believe I could ascend Mt. Everest with more balance, agility, and dignity than I can climb bleachers. Fortunately, on the night of the concert, the only available seating space was in the back of the gym, so only half the audience saw me sprawl over the third bleacher, with both arms out-flung to catch myself.

At the close of the program, the entire family rushed to my side to make sure there would not be a repeat of my previous performance.

Do I mind that they'll remember the Christmas of 1991 as the year Grandma fell up the bleachers? No. Laughter is part of the cumulative process.

In the van on the way home, the children were impressed when I told them that Martha, their six-year-old cousin, was right then playing Mary in the manger scene in her Alabama church pageant. Knowing her reputation for being a bit unpredictable (I call the quality "spontaneous and exciting"), they expressed hope that she would be demure and properly reserved in the portrayal of her role.

Yes, Christmas is cumulative.

From all over, messages have come this year. A call from Kentucky this morning informed me that my sister has a new granddaughter. The obstetrician had thought she would need to be a Caesarean baby, but she announced her plans to arrive at nine in the morning and entered the outside world, all on her own, only three hours later, just in time for lunch. The Christmas season is conducive to miracles.

A long-time friend in Colorado wrote to tell me that her fifteen-year-old grandson who has been diagnosed with a fatal liver disease had finally become financially eligible to be placed on the liver transplant donor list. Ben's classmates had raised around fifty thousand dollars to help with the staggering surgical and hospital expenses.

Enclosed in a card from a former student was a beautiful poem, actually a thrilling eulogy that she had composed to honor her father while he is still here to lead an active, fruitful life. She should never have thanked me for inspiring her; it was she who made me see music and beauty in words.

When I take dishes to help a friend with refreshments at a meeting or party, I often carelessly forget to bring them home. Two glass bowls had been returned to me, and when I unwrapped them this morning, there on top lay a glass dome with a royal blue sky and Santa astride a pacing reindeer. Nothing quite equals the magic of turning the dome upside down and watching the snowflakes swirl.

Right before lunch, a neighbor brought a fat, round pine tree to fit the table in the corner of the thirteen-foot ceiling living room. As far as my Christmas trees are concerned, Christmas Present has recently won out over Christmas Past. Years ago, while our children were growing up, to settle for a tree on a table was unthinkable. The evergreen had to brush the ceiling, or at least the angel's halo did, but now all seem satisfied with a tree that is just as impressive on the old, round mahogany table and far simpler to dismantle.

As I wrapped packages this afternoon, one of the dairymen on the farm stopped in to tell me, "Don't worry about wood for the kitchen stove during Christmas. We just split some elm that will really put out the heat."

From the upstairs hall tonight, the moon is full and gorgeous, clearly outlining the silhouettes of bare trees and wire fences that have bordered the fields for more than fifty years.

It's true that farmers have quietly dreaded the rapid spread of the housing developments. They love the land and feel strongly that we must preserve it to feed this country, but I'll have to admit it's comforting to look out my window tonight and see the sprinkling of house lights. Some homes are brilliant with multi-colored strings of lights, some with plain single candles glowing in the windows. Somehow, despite differences in lifestyles, even though I've never met some of the people, even though they live nearly a half mile away, in the glow of Christmas lights, I feel "close."

Perhaps you're thinking, "Have all your so-called 'cumulative' pre-holiday experiences been so pleasant?" Oh, no! One day last week I worked so hard, accomplished so little, lost my wrapping tape three times, discovered I had bought the wrong size undershirts, found I had made a one-hundred-dollar mistake in my checkbook (not in my favor), my Christmas exuberance flew out the window faster than Santa's sleigh dashed over the rooftop. I was almost happy when I smashed the forefinger on my right hand because it gave me a chance to sit down and shed some legitimate tears. The ugly nail still makes an excellent conversation piece, and estimates of the time it will take to come off range from New Year's Eve to Christmas 1992.

Yes, like you, no doubt, I attempt too much, get uptight, and forget what Christmas is all about. Then I turn on the television and watch Jessica Tandy in "The Story Lady," or play my Mormon Tabernacle Choir cassette that contains "Silent Night,", and once again I realize "All is calm, all is bright."

Our cumulative Christmas seasons are progressive, related thoughts of loved ones, music, the glow of a star in the East, red poinsettia plants on a church altar, the quietness of a morning snow flurry and the realization that even though the world is in sad shape today, it could be far worse had a child not been born in a Bethlehem manger nearly two thousand years ago. It would be worse because we would not have hope to cling to.

This Christmas morning Jim won't be hurrying in from the barn to open gifts and to linger with me over a late breakfast, but I am grateful that he could hurry in for so many years.

Our children will be with their own children in their own homes, and that is as it should be. Yes, this Christmas morning I'll be here in the old farmhouse by myself, but not for a moment will I be alone.

Winter on the Farm

The dinner bell on the smokehouse still sounds,
and the old truck still runs.

Quality Time

If only I hadn't already put stamps on the envelopes! Every January check had been dated 1991. Not until I signed the check for my car insurance premium did I realize I was a whole year behind. Disgusted with my absentmindedness, I examined the half dozen envelopes to determine whether or not I dare risk opening them, changing 1991 to 1992, and resealing them. I doubted it because a shredder in a large, industrial office doesn't do any more damage to a glued envelop flap than I generally do.

Anyway, how could another year have gone by so quickly? I know this January came sooner than the last one. I know I'll hardly catch my breath before another spring is here. Honestly, the grass outside this window never turned brown all last winter. My birthdays are coming every six months now!

I read the other day that metabolically, time does go faster as we age. Whether the concept is biological or psychological, I often wish I could reach out and hold back a few years. There is so much yet to be done! Most mornings when I wake I don't wonder, "What can I do today?" I am fortunate! Instead, I wonder, "What must I eliminate if I can't get everything done?"

Still undecided about the sealed, stamped envelopes and still musing over the paramount importance of time in our lives — often a tyrant, then again a helpmate — I notice the square box beside me on my desk. Inside the box, on royal blue velvet, is a wrist watch, elegant in design, exquisite in detail. The brand is internationally known, the band woven of tightly meshed gold, the face black so I can better see the numbers with my imperfect vision. The twelve and six digits are diamonds; clouds have covered the sun this January morning, but the gems pick up the glow of the desk lamp and sparkle.

My thoughts wander back through the years, and suddenly it dawns on me that I have never bought myself a watch.

In high school I didn't own one; very few of my classmates did. We didn't need a watch to tell us when to catch the school bus. We didn't hurry to a fast food place for work at four o'clock because there weren't any fast food places. Earl, the handsome, dark-haired senior who drove us to school in his blue Plymouth, did own a watch. One year when a flash flood completely wiped out the county road, he drove down the creek bed. I didn't need a time piece then, for I could hear his tires crunching on the rocks. That was the year the song "Winter Wonderland" came out, and Earl serenaded us in his smooth baritone all during the two mile trip to school — on time!

When I entered junior college at the county seat, Mother insisted that I take her watch that she had purchased when she was teaching during the last year of World War I. With cleaning and a new winding stem, it performed flawlessly. She wanted to give it to me, but I'm glad I just borrowed it because she needed it when she returned to teaching during World War II.

I didn't buy my first watch, but I worked hard for it. When I entered college, I was young both chronologically and socially; in reality, I was a prime candidate for Heartbreak.

Each year the junior college valedictorian was awarded a wrist watch decorated with two diamonds. I don't recall having that award as a goal, but I thought I might have a chance, until I fell for the tall Tennesseean who called me "Carrot Top" with soft, Southern "r's." My chronological and social immaturity surfaced; common sense flew out the campus windows. My associates seemed very much concerned about the seriousness of the relationship. I still shudder when I remember the night the petite, precise Dean of Women came into my dormitory room and warned me that if I didn't stop spending all Sunday afternoons sitting on the back chapel steps with my gallant, southern hero, my grade average would surely descend to deplorable depths. Worse still, when the owner of the general store where my dad bought groceries casually commented, "I hear Odessa is about to get married," I'll never forget what happened. On the following Sunday afternoon, while my hero and I were sitting on the front steps of the Administrative Building (Chapel steps off limits), here came Daddy in his tan, 1929 Model A Ford. He had driven twenty-five miles over three mountains of winding curves to find out "what was going on." I remember he was kind.

When I did receive the watch on graduation morning, I was thrilled, but not because I could say, "See, you all were wrong," or "I showed you." My grades were far from good in some subjects. I won't reveal my art grade, and most likely the reason I won the watch was because the only math required in the two-year course was teacher's arithmetic. I know now I had to prove to myself that I could be more than a visually impaired girl who managed to do fairly well academically, that I could be like any other school girl who fell foolishly but normally in love. That year I grew up.

I'll admit it took me many months to recover from my broken heart when the Tennesseean's attentions turned to someone else (can you believe another redhead?), but the watch was there to console me and to tick away promises of future, more lasting romances.

The college watch directed my routine for thirty years. Suddenly one day, while I was teaching a fifth-period, eleventh-grade-English class, it stopped — not as dramatically as Grandfather's clock that stopped when the old man died — but quietly and permanently. I jokingly told my students the watch's history, including the drama on the chapel steps, the Model A Ford, and the broken heart.

They laughed with me, and they sympathized with me. Some of them had already found out what it was like, as they termed it, "to be dumped."

About a week later I instructed the same English class at the beginning of the period to open their grammar workbooks. I even remember the page number — forty. No one moved. I repeated the instruction. Still, not a book was opened. Instead, John rose quietly from his seat in the center of the classroom. I noticed a small, brown paper bag in his hand. As he walked toward the front, he said, "Maybe you'd better sit down, Mrs. Snyder." Puzzled, I obeyed. The class waited silently as he handed me the bag and told me, "Open it." Inside lay a box with a local jeweller's label. In it was a watch — oval-shaped, dainty, lovely, not at all inexpensive. I knew the brand name, but the maker didn't matter. What mattered was that it was given to me with love from seventeen precious young people.

A few weeks ago I realized my English class' gift of the late 1960s was fast tiring out. Perhaps it sensed it was time to bow to the quartz theory of operation and to retire, along with the college watch, to the special memory corner of my musical jewelry box that plays "'I Could Have Danced All Night."

While a very close teacher friend and I were reminiscing recently, I happened to mention how sentimental I felt about a possession so reliable and loyal. I was not hinting. I fully intended to buy myself a cheap, everyday watch to make sure I was on time for my beauty parlor appointments. I wouldn't object to one I had to wind every day.

Christmas Eve I opened the friend's gift.

Few times in my life have I been speechless. Many times I've said the wrong things, but speechless? No! There lay the blue box now on the desk behind me.

I searched for words to thank my friend of many years — overwhelmed, unbelievable, undeserving, why — no exclamations or questions fit. Finally, to her I said, "There is no way I can thank you." Quietly, she replied, "You know you are welcome." She is such an honest, sincere person I somehow knew I *was* welcome! I stopped asking "Why?"

I still haven't decided whether or not to leave the checks dated 1991, but out of my rambling thoughts on this gray, January morning has come a brilliant and comforting revelation:

How can I complain about the years slipping by so fast when I have already been blessed with so much "Quality Time"?

Tears and Laughter: A Valentine Story

One of the most life-threatening illnesses when I was a child was referred to as "double" pneumonia. Fearfully, loved ones waited for what they called the "crisis." I remember a statement frequently made by some of the old-timers; it was not a consoling conclusion, merely a fact. They would say with emphasis, "You have to hit the bottom before you can start to climb back up!"

That theory can apply in many situations other than the much-feared pneumonia of days before penicillin.

Jim, my husband, passed away five years ago this month. Two days before he died, he and I had laughed and talked together for hours in the hospital intensive care unit. Actually, it was our most delightful Valentine's Day in all our forty years together. The unexpected heart attack of the day before had tested to be moderate, and all signs pointed toward his resuming a normal, active life. He wrote special notes on valentines to his grandchildren, calling the mischievous one "the cutest little rascal I ever saw". Calmly he admitted he wouldn't be up to planting his vegetable garden that spring, but he was sure he could do his flowers.

When I handed him the corny valentine I had bought him, I clumsily knocked against the concealed wires that controlled the monitoring machines. I remember my panic when I glanced toward the bed. What a relief to know the problem! All afternoon we laughed about it. He commented that he had always known I was clumsy, but usually I only endangered myself, not someone else!

The same problem with the monitors happened two days later, but it was real this time, and I'm so glad I wasn't there. The Valentine laughter was only a memory.

When the before dawn call came from the hospital, I stood frozen. Two things I shall never forget. How our son realized what I needed most to hear, I'll never know. His first words when he reached me from up across the fields were, "Mom, in all of this, do exactly what you want to do. We've always known you and Dad had something special."

How could he have known that I could not go to the hospital for his dad's personal belongings? How could he know that next morning I could not go to the funeral home to check on final arrangements? He and his loyal aunt went both times. I chose the music and reminded them to include shasta daisies in the flower arrangement — that was all.

Then — I'll always remember our daughter Beth's first words when she arrived the afternoon of his death: "Mom, we all know that as long as there's a flower that blooms, Pop will be here."

All through the hazy days that followed, so many stood by — family, friends, church, community — so many to lean on, quietly doing the little caring things that kept me going. They told me they were proud of my courage. But I knew the real impact had not come! I was drifting, floating aimlessly and dreamily without direction, clinging to those I loved, drawing strength from them, but in my mind, I knew the darkest moments lay somewhere in the uncharted times ahead.

Not many days after the funeral, Beth mentioned that she had to attend an industrial conference in Washington, D.C. Thomas, my son-in-law, had planned to accompany her, but he could not leave his research project. The hotel room was already reserved. An added bonus at the seminar would be dinner at the British Embassy. Would I — could I go? The family and I conferred, and we agreed it might be good therapy.

We did go, and no part of the experience was a disappointment.

One note of interest — not a pleasant one — I could look out my hotel window and see the exact site of the attempted assassination of President Reagan. Also, I could watch limousines pull up at the entrance, see immaculately uniformed chauffeurs assist visitors in designer clothes into the breezeway. Different from my world? Yes. Therapy? I wasn't sure.

Next day saw an incongruous pattern. While Beth attended meetings, I sat in the spacious lounge in a comfortable chair and wrote thank-you notes. Periodically, I glanced up to see stylishly dressed professionals parade by to their scientific meetings. Yes, I was able to write. Certainly I could not complete the task; so many had done so much.

That night we truly entered a different world. A London style, double-decker bus (all British personnel) picked us up at the hotel and took us a longer, scenic route to the Embassy building. The entire affair was low-keyed and lovely — an enormous, semi-circular banquet table loaded with luscious dishes, a chamber orchestra adding softness and depth to the atmosphere. The British men (some with their wives) blended easily with all of us, seeking out individuals just to chat.

One handsome computer specialist inquired if I had ever done public relations work, adding that I seemed to communicate so easily. I thought, "Oh yes, right now I'm doing an expert PR job on myself! I'm smiling, I'm mingling, I'm probably doing an acting job worthy of Hollywood. I'm hiding the heartbreak, moving about in a whole new world totally foreign to my dairy farm life style. Maybe I could have been a PR lady!"

We were no more than half way home the next day when I felt the letdown creep in, when I was tempted to ask Beth to turn around and take me anywhere but back to the farm. I tried hard to conceal the despair stealing over me, but she knew.

We walked through the kitchen, on into the big family room. Jim's black chair sat where it had been for years — an ugly chair, ungraceful in its contours, but he was comfortable in it.

Then the darkness came — the torrents, the pent up hurt, the feeling of deep inconsolable loss. I leaned against the door frame and sobbed — not cried — wrenching, tearing sounds. I remember Beth whispering, "Mom, I guess I took you away too soon."

But she didn't! This time had to come. I knew later that the temporary vacation from grief was good.

First, it proved to me that no matter how deep our personal losses are, the world does go on. People, not only guests at a British Embassy dinner, but even our loved ones do go on living. They have to — and they should!

And second, when I leaned against the door frame and vented the hurt and emptiness inside me, I hit, as people say, "rock bottom." In the grief process, the lowest level can later be a source of strength, a kind of gauge for what lies ahead. During the months that followed, and even yet being halfway home and suddenly realizing he isn't there has been the hardest part of the healing. And yet, so many times when that empty feeling begins to sneak in, I have thought, "It couldn't be any worse than the first time I came back home. I made it then; I'll make it now."

Beth need never feel guilty about taking me away from reality. That coming home was the first step in the healing process.

I firmly believe the same old saying that applied to the crisis in double pneumonia applies easily to grief over a loved one, and possibly to countless other life situations. You *do* have to hit the bottom before you can begin to climb back up.

The climbing was slow and tortuous, but quite some time ago, I noticed that I was remembering the valentine laughter more often and more vividly than the homecoming tears!

Not Long 'Til Planting Time

No kindling is better than crisp, dry locust bark. All winter it has helped keep my kitchen cozy warm. This morning I drove to a spot near the center of the farm where the men had sawed down a tall locust tree and filled my car trunk with long slivers of bark.

Yesterday's chilly wind had calmed; the sun felt almost warm after my stooping exertion, and for several moments, I just stood quietly. Fields lay around me in all directions, 400 acres of land. I thought, "How quickly the seasons go! Soon it will be planting time again — these fields that have been planted for close to two centuries. This year, will my son plant alfalfa here? Barley over there? Corn in the unusually fertile fields along the highway?"

My thoughts wandered back close to twenty years, to the day our son graduated from college with a math degree. On the way home from the ceremony, Nick said to me, "Mom, I can never go inside and work".

If I said I was elated by the announcement, I would not be telling the truth. I was a teacher; I loved living on the farm but had never participated in sustaining it. His dad was the planter, the tiller, the harvester, the parent close to the land. Somehow, when Nick expressed his wishes for the future, memories of all the good times did a temporary fadeout. Instead, I recalled the late suppers, the vacations not taken, embarrassing moments when we walked into church long after the opening hymn, corn tassels stunted and scorched in hot, summer sun, milk dumped into piles of snow because the milk truck couldn't get in the drifted, mile-long lane, the seasons of meager crops and lean cash flow. No, I was not too thrilled on our son's graduation day when I knew he would become a fourth generation farmer in the Snyder family.

During that summer, however, one remote incident enlightened me. While sorting his college materials, I came across a composition he had written in an English class. I doubt that he knows I kept it. I'd like to quote a few paragraphs from it:

> The summers are still hot but not as warm to my memory as those of the 1950s. My childhood spanned that decade, and to a lad living on a farm, the summer was constant excitement. Those were days when school was forgotten but learning continued, for every day there was something new to consider on the farm.
>
> Even with the machinery the work was hard. It doesn't take long to tire while lifting thirty-pound bales of hay all day long, and I was completely exhausted many times. It

was a different kind of exhaustion from that I feel today, though.

I would look over the barren strip in the field where the hay had been, and a tremendous sense of accomplishment would come over me. From somewhere I would get enough energy to go bicycling or ground-hog hunting in the late evening. There was no worry about what I had to do next day because my father was cooking up something, and I would be eager to help.

Things changed as I grew up. I began to realize that one strip of hay taken in meant that it was time to cut more hay to take in. No, my summers are not like they used to be, for now there is an element of concern not found in small boys.

Even so, warm memories of those summers still serve as a bracer whenever I am having trouble with the world today.

I remember thinking after I first read the paper, "Why wouldn't a mother want for her child a career that could serve as a 'bracer' for him?"

Don't misunderstand me. I'm not saying, "From that day when I read the paper, I have been glad he chose farming as a career." I'm sure that many times he, too, has questioned the wisdom of his decision, but he persevered and worked hard. In the meantime, his mother watched and learned. Mothers can learn, you know, especially when there's a nagging thought that her judgment might have been faulty.

From the beginning, he and I both knew that the career he chose faced powerful negative forces. In fact, along with rare animals and exotic plants, the small farm is fast becoming an endangered species.

Certainly, farming on any scale is controlled more rigidly by natural phenomena than most other occupations. The planter hopes for three out of five good, or even moderate, years; possibly, he can ride the waves with two out of five. He survives both because of Nature and in spite of it.

His outgo is staggering. Aggravating the problem is a formidable adversary — the lack of public knowledge, which, in turn, breeds indifference. The supermarket customer probably never knows that the farmer often pays his workers more per week than he keeps for his own family. The farmer fervently hopes that in spring planting, none of the oversize, rear tires on any of the tractors blows out; his family could live for two weeks on the amount he would have to pay for that one tire!

As a dairyman, my son feels that he has to plant corn for silage and for the grain bank. He does some quick calculating — let's see, considering spray material, fertilizer, seed, equipment operation, labor — what is the cost per acre? He is so stunned he calculates a second time, but unfortunately, the first total was correct.

However, neither Nature nor outgo is the root of the farmer's dilemma. These problems he could handle — work around — if he were fairly paid for what he produced. Even though retail cost of practically every item from the necessary to the frivolous has tripled since the 1970s, last year my son was paid per bushel of corn one third less than his dad received in 1975.

He hates to admit it, but he has long since given up trying to unravel the mystery of why he is being so grossly underpaid for his produce (even the milk on which his entire economy is based), so he, like many others in the field, searched for a plan to off-set the problem.

Increasing production seemed a logical solution.

Sadly, though, if he increases production, the word "surplus" can begin to hang over his head like a double-edged sword, and he has learned that too often, the claims of those existing surpluses are not legitimate. Down his prices tumble, and he suddenly finds that he is planting more acreage, milking more cows, and making less money! All along he wonders, "How can there be a surplus when so many in this world are hungry for what I need to sell?"

Also, increasing production can create an undesirable by-product. He has no time to improve his capital investment. The sun is low over the western hill before he realizes he hasn't had a minute to clean the fence rows, repair the barn roof, paint the silage wagon, brush hog the thistles, scrape the graveled lane for the eighteen-wheeler milk truck, caulk the west windows in his dwelling house. The dream of building a machine shed to reduce equipment depreciation has long since vanished — not enough cash and not enough time.

No doubt you are asking, "After your depressing (and honestly, I am not by nature a pessimist) picture of the endangered species, why have your son and others like him stayed on the land?"

The reasons are surprisingly simple and vitally important:

> Early the farmer learns that Nature is basically kind. An old poem says, "For every cloudy morning, there's a midnight moon above." Also a theologian declared, "No mortal has more faith than a farmer." When the severe drought threatened Nick's corn crop last summer, I heard him say, "If my corn crop fails, I'll plant sudex later."

After a long, dry spell, all memories of lean years and crop failures fade when he wakes one morning to the sound of rain on the roof.

The farmer finds his work a challenge. When milk prices failed to rise, Nick concentrated on improving the dairy feed formula. His efforts paid off.

As he drives his red pickup down to the dairy in early morning, he notices a cow has quietly had her calf during the night — a heifer, too!

He says to a neighbor during a good season, "I can't believe I've already gotten three cuttings of alfalfa off this field this year," and the neighbor says, "My barley has really turned out well."

His children now live in the old, rambling farmhouse with the sloping floors and clawfoot bathtub that their great-great grandfather lived in — roots, continuity, so sorely needed now!

I cannot produce statistics to verify my statement, but I strongly believe that the family farm is the most cohesive single unit in American society today.

Speaking of cohesiveness, in late evening, thirteen-year-old Kevin, wearing coveralls like his dad's, forks out hay bales (huge, round ones now) to feed the cattle; Mimi, the mom, bottle feeds a baby calf that was rejected by his mother; eleven-year-old Natalie watches the casserole in the oven; Eric, the eight-year-old, waters the heifers (his salary is still $3.50 per week, the same as last year). All five will be in for a 7:30 sitdown, family supper at an old, oak table they recently refinished in their "spare time."

The fourth generation family farm is quiet for the night.

Before I turned my car around and headed for home after loading the locust bark, I again glanced over the fields and knew they would soon be plowed for planting.

Those dark, rich furrows could very well be the lifeline of this country.

I am so glad that out son, and others like him, couldn't go inside and work!

Voices of the Very Young

The voice on the phone sounded despondent, close to tears.

"Grandma, I hate to tell you, but I got in trouble at school today."

Our third grader does get in trouble at home sometimes but seldom at school.

"What happened, Honey?" — fearfully.

"I got in a fight on the playground."

"Did you have to go to the office?"

"Yes." I thought I heard a sniffle.

"Have you told your mom and dad?"

"No, not yet."

Then there was a pause followed by a roar of laughter and the "in" word of the younger set now, "Psych, I just made all that up to see what you would say."

Later, I learned that today's children had changed the dictionary word "psych" to a simpler, comic book spelling "sike," but it still means, "Goody, I fooled you!"

I am at present plotting revenge.

Incidents such as the above have convinced me that our young can be extremely proficient with the spoken word. I would say that my grandson could be either an actor or a con artist.

An experience not long ago taught me that the young are also quite skilled with the written language.

Since most of my teaching years were spent in senior high school, I must admit I was a trifle apprehensive when I faced sixty sixth graders on a recent afternoon at South Jefferson Elementary School. My assignment was to make them want to write, to do a motivational lesson in creative writing for their Language Arts Class.

From the beginning, I questioned my plans. I wanted them to do actual, "in-class" writing, but when I realized there were three classes of sixth graders, I envisioned at least two-thirds of them sitting cross-legged on the floor, writing on a flimsy folder or possibly, on the carpet. That problem was solved. Forty students carried their part-metal desks, the interiors crammed with four or five heavy textbooks, down the hall and placed them in a regular sized classroom already containing at least twenty other desks. I have since regretted that I did not take my camera to preserve the image of that unusual procession. After the complicated mechanics of fitting the desks in (a surprisingly quiet procedure), the students sat so close to me that I could have reached out and touched at least two dozen of them. I found the closeness comforting.

I doubted my time element. Remembering that the average interest span of many college students is twenty-three minutes, I shivered to think of holding those eleven and twelve-year-olds for over an hour.

I shouldn't have worried.

A teacher raised a hand into the air and a hush fell. I don't recall an actual command — or reprimand — during the entire time span. I marvelled at the way the three teachers exercised a kind of silent, gentle control that seemed based not on threats, but on unspoken expectations.

Nor do I recall any moans or groans when I asked them to write — anything, in any form — a paragraph, a page, a poem, song lyrics — just write!

I suggested possible topics: "Full Moon", "Why?", "All By Myself", but they could also choose their own.

Jennifer chose "All By Myself" and enhanced it with an element of contrast:

> When I'm all by myself, sometimes I feel lonely, like there is something missing.

Sometimes when the house is empty
and I'm alone, I feel like crying.
Sometimes when I'm all by myself I
feel my heart is broken into a million
pieces
But sometimes when I'm all by myself
I feel happy like a bird freed from its
cage!

I'm glad when young people realize that "alone time" is essential for peace of mind and an important part of character building.

During the writing period, Rocky asked "Why?":

Why does the sun shine?
Why do birds fly?
Why is the sky blue?
Why, why am I at this moment
wondering what's going to happen
tomorrow?
Why did God put us on this beautiful,
bountiful land?
Why have many gone before us to
another world and left us in grief and
sorrow?
Why are people so blind that they do
evil things?
Why? — so much I need to know!

How fortunate for all generations that even the very young ask "Why?"!

Tim chose his own titles, and they are quite intriguing; his conclusions probe deeply into important facets of living:

Frozen Days

Days that stand still -
Days that don't exist, and
Stand with nothing, like a block of ice
Because time has passed us by.

Time

It's time to realize that we have to change
And live a life of good,
If we don't, before and beyond us
Time builds a barrier of steel and wood.

Truth

Truth is a spring of Faith
Truth is the Wind of Time
It is also a leap of Hope,
And to turn to lies is a Waste

Life

Life is a bottled up dream,
Life can be nothing but a puff of smoke,
Don't wait until it's gone
To know how good it is!

Mark creates a restful, contemplative mood in sentences that shine with imagery:

Full Moon

The moon creeps up on the silhouetted evergreen trees as the crickets rub their legs together, almost making a spark.

The moon shows the majestic deer prancing on the silent confetti that lies on the ground, sparkling as if the moon were a spotlight.

The glittering stars gently tap the moon on their way across the blue ocean of never-ending conifers that have been covered with the purest of sugars.

A ticking time bomb — the moon — ready to explode the night into the busy, lighted world of the living — the silence is over, at least until another full moon.

In February, I participated in a Board of Education Language Arts Fair involving the entire county.

Again I saw bright eyes and mirrored thoughts. Yesterday, an added bonus came to me in the mail. Two Shepherdstown first graders made my day when I opened an envelope and read Mellisa's poem "My Friend."

My friend is fun,
We play in the sun,
She shines so bright,
She's my guiding light.

Underneath was a sketch of the sun with a star close by.

Lindsey entitled her poem "Stars."

Stars twinkle in the night and
They make a pretty sight.
When they glitter
You will see, oh, how pretty
they can be!

Later, I thought, "If first graders think about friends, the sun and the stars, we who are supposed to lead them must shed some of our pessimism and fears about the future, and like those very young, begin to *Look Up*!"

I had been asked to encourage and inspire these young people to express openly what they feel inside.

The role was reversed; they encouraged and inspired me!

The Spice of Life

If the old saying "Variety is the spice of life" is reliable, I'm in deep trouble as far as my body nourishment is concerned.

I could count the number of foods I can eat on my ten fingers; I wouldn't need to use any of my toes. Every day (holidays, too) I eat exactly the same foods, the same amounts, prepared in the same way and at about the same time. I refer to it as my "same" diet.

You're probably wanting to ask, "Are you trying to regain your youthful, curvaceous figure?" I never had a youthful, curvaceous figure. Maybe it's best that silicone wasn't available back then; I might have been tempted to try it!

Normal people could be helped if their lower intestinal muscles were, as my doctors describe the malady, "in a state of disarray," but my extreme medicine intolerance prevents proper treatment. Reactions to medications have many times proved more unbearable than the original discomfort or the "same" diet.

Even relatives and friends have declared they could not bear to eat the same food day in and day out. I think they could if their appetites happened to be as healthy as mine. I'm very grateful for that.

Perhaps you think the diet is tolerable because I never did eat much. You are wrong! All my life I have loved to eat, and I have liked everything but seafood with an oily, fishy taste.

My dad was a railroad man, but other than his family, his gardening gave him his greatest joy. Jim, my husband, was a dairyman, but his finest hours were spent in his garden — so believe me, I did eat!

Do I ever have a craving, though, for a special food or just a touch of variety? Oh, yes! — especially in the springtime. I've even wished a Genie with magic healing powers would appear and tell me that even for a short time, I could eat what I wanted. What would I choose?

Certainly, I would want some of my dad's little, half-runner, green beans. He planted them between the rows of field corn back on the hill. They required spreading room, and the mountain was steep enough to form a kind of terrace for them. Mother cooked them with bacon drippings and served them with pork backbone and cornbread. Her cornbread was slightly on the heavy side because she used neither egg nor sugar, but the iron skillet baked such beautiful, golden crusts, one ignored the inside.

Also, I'd like one of Daddy's long, slender sweet potatoes, baked unpeeled and later split open and spread with homemade, Jersey cow butter.

When I was growing up, setting out sweet potatoes was a major family project. Daddy grew his own "slips" in a board-enclosed, mulched bed. When they reached the proper height, he built up a long ridge across the garden with a wide hoe, then raked the dirt smooth on top. My job later was to take the end of the hoe handle and gouge a hole about every twelve inches along the top of the ridge. Usually, my spacing was fairly accurate. My middle sister then came along with a bucket of water and a blue, granite dipper and filled the holes. Our baby sister had the easy job. All she had to do was take a handful of plants, separate them gently, and drop one in each water-filled hole. Daddy performed the final task. He, with his fingers and the palms of his hands, gathered moist dirt up around the plants, filled in the hole, and patted the soil into a smooth mound. By then, Mother would call out the kitchen window that supper was ready.

I wouldn't know what to choose from the gardens Jim used to grow. Maybe I would break off new, green lettuce leaves, add chopped boiled eggs, bacon bits, and a few slivers of spring onion, then toss with homemade salad dressing.

I realize it's disgracefully wasteful to dig tiny, new, white potatoes, but I'd do it anyway and cover them with melted butter and sprigs of parsley. Jim's baby beets were so good, too, and they added color to the menu. Hopefully, there would still be some of his new brand of sugar peas, not the snow peas nor the snap peas —

they're good, but how sweet and succulent the sugar peas are! I always liked the ordinary, old-time peas if someone else picked them and shelled them. There seemed to be so much volume depreciation from the plant to the cooking pot.

If the Genie granted my request later in the season, I would want an ear of white corn, a large slice of yellow tomato, some broccoli flowerlets I had snapped from the stalk, and by all means, pole limas. What a treat they were! It was so exciting to poke my head into the wigwam structures that held them and pluck the long beans from the vine. Meat loaf made from Shenstone Farm's extra lean hamburger would add the final culinary touch.

If the Genie appeared in late fall or early winter, I know what I'd ask for. Have you ever eaten salsify? Some call it "oyster plant" because there is about it a faint flavor of oysters. It's a late vegetable with slender roots like a carrot but pearly white in color. Jim used to say, "It's good but you earn every bite of it." It's difficult to dig because the hairy roots plunge deep down and cling tenaciously to the soil. Don' t be upset if you leave half of it chopped off underground. Also, if you plan to go anywhere within the next few days, have some bleach handy. Even if you use a carrot scrapper to prepare it, your hands turn an unsightly purplish-brown. Should the Genie allow me salsify, I would dice it, boil it tender, layer it in a casserole dish with salt and pepper, cover with milk and dabs of oleo, then top with cracker crumbs and bake.

Of course all the above is wishful thinking, but I must admit that from the disarrayed muscles and preposterous diet, I have learned so much.

First, I have learned to improvise. Grape jelly and 50 percent fat-free margarine layered between two crackers makes a tasty dessert. My three youngest grandchildren rank that combination their number one request on the snack menu.

Also, last month my doctor announced to me, "You are seventy years old," — I didn't need to be reminded of that — "but your last blood work was that of a twenty-year-old!" I'll admit will power didn't accomplish all that; vitamin and mineral supplements helped.

Then, too, since a year ago, I have gained a whole pound. Who knows? — I might graduate from "bony" to "slender" on the figure scale; even "skinny" would sound healthier than "bony."

After living all these years, it took the "same" diet to teach me a valuable lesson: You can do almost anything in life if you know you have to. But most important, I have learned that variety doesn't have to be the spice of life if we still have an appetite for food — and for living!

It's supper time now. I'll go poach my egg. I like poached eggs, always did, and my cholesterol is a safe 196.

Besides, after writing this article, I'm hungry enough to eat anything!

Just a Matter of Time

What I say, no doubt, does sound strange to my eleven-year-old granddaughter.

"Goodbye, Old House. I'll be back."

She asks, "Do you always say that when you leave home?"

"Yes."

"Why?"

"So it'll know I'll be back."

As the tall, thirteen-year-old grandson carries out the last piece of luggage, he comments, "Sure is going to be peaceful around here, but I'll miss my snacks."

The van is loaded and ready to go. Grandma is leaving for a visit with the other grandchildren in Alabama.

Dad does a last minute check at the dairy barn. Mom takes the driver's seat. Six fit easily into the van. Grandma can even stretch out her skinny legs on the ledge in front of her. Eric, the eight-year-old, has ample space for his bag of books. As we settle into our positions, I glance into the back seat and the thought occurs to me, "It's so good that Kevin, as tall as his father, and Natalie, already taller than Grandma, are here."

Soon — almost too soon — they will be going separate ways, finding their own destinies, too busy molding their own futures to go on many family trips.

It's nearly noon already, but it doesn't seem to matter that we have close to 450 miles to go — all the way to Tennessee to meet my daughter and her son. Deadlines don't seem to matter as much on a warm, spring day.

Down the Shenandoah Valley in bright, April sunshine — about the same time we spot the redbuds blooming along the roadside, the sunshine turns into warm rain. Mimi, my daughter-in-law, mentions that she smelled the rain long before it hit the windshield. My son Nick, the dairy farmer, notes, "I hope we're getting this up home. Have to get that corn in the ground."

Someone hums the first few bars of the hypnotic song "Shenandoah." The children (even the youngest) know that the real Shenandoah is not the valley but an Indian chief whose daughter was loved by a white man somewhere in Missouri River country.

I add that when Grandpa and I got engaged forty-four years ago, the football team in the Kentucky school where I taught serenaded me (unharmoniously) on a school bus when we were returning from a victory in a nearby county — and yes, Eric, they did have football teams back then!

Dad, his feed store, billed cap pulled down over his eyes to protect them from the sun that has reappeared, snoozes in the front passenger seat.

We cruise by exit signs with names of old valley towns. I mention that on several Sunday afternoon outings, Grandpa and I used to drive through here, not on the spread out super highway, but on the road that runs parallel through the center of the many one-traffic-light communities. I'm now reminded of a quieter time when going fast didn't matter so much.

No one seems to tire, especially after being fortified with an apple fritter lunch. Late afternoon fades into twilight. No one seems to mind that we will be hitting a totally unfamiliar city after dark, searching for a totally unfamiliar hotel. Besides, the full, mellow moon has risen. This moon is not a silver one; it looks like a bright yellow sun that has gradually faded into a soft, creamy yellow.

An hour after dark we spot our city signs, and after only one wrong turn that is quickly rectified by advice from a young man in a mini-mart, we pull into the underground, hotel parking lot.

As we enter the hotel lobby, we hear the piano in the second level dining room. Someone is playing "Don't Get Around Much Anymore." To the other two generations in the crew, the song might not mean much, but Grandma relives the 1940s all over again.

Beth, the daughter, and Jimmy, the long-legged, curly-haired nine-year-old, are already here. Martha, the seven-year-old, and her dad are waiting at home in Alabama.

Such a reunion! From Christmas to Easter is a long time for a parent and child, brother, sister and sister-in-law, cousins not to see each other.

No, Grandma isn't going down to the swimming pool. No, she's not interested in the heated whirlpool, either. She didn't bring her bathing suit. She has used that excuse many times, but the real excuse is she has never even owned a bathing suit. A grin spreads across the face of the thirteen-year-old, and I hear, "I can see why!"

Is Grandma tired? Not really. Still, it's inviting to turn back the bed cover, put the hot-pink satin pillow case on the hotel pillow. It's supposed to protect the hairdo, but Grandma is not living proof of that.

On into the night two large pizzas are delivered, and talk overpowers the pay movie on the television screen.

The bed feels good, but on Shenstone Farm, I fall asleep hearing only the sounds of night birds or a bawling calf. No sleep for me yet, not with the chatter and laughter of seven people in an average size hotel room, three bright lamps burning, and the tantalizing aroma of pizza. I hear from them next morning that I was in deep sleep at least two hours before the party broke up and the extras left for the additional hotel room.

Next morning our destination, after driving several miles out of the city, is a mountain top. We begin the climb. Many trees are beginning to put on their lacy greenery, but the pines stand stately and dignified and seem to say, "So what? I've been green all winter." Clouds weave in and out overhead, occasionally covering the sun but not for long. The warm rains have already reached here, for the creek that plays hide-and-seek with us, first on one side of the road then the other, is full. Yes, we all agree, the most captivating of all the natural splendors around us is the creek. The water is clear and sparkling, foamy in the rapids, slow-moving in the tranquil places, and almost always rocky. They are beautiful, smooth rocks, some boulder size leaning against the banks, some clustered in stepping stone fashion in the water. A younger grandson expresses the urge to walk across the stream on the stepping stones, but the older one reminds him the water would freeze his toes, not only in April but in mid-July.

We drive the twenty miles slowly, not because the van lacks pulling power with eight passengers, but because there is so much to see.

And then the climax of the trip — the highway ends, but not the journey. Ahead of us is the thirty-degree trail climb — on up one-half mile (I believe the surveyors underestimated the distance) to the top where the observation tower promises a treat not only for the occupants of vehicles but also for the hikers on the Appalachian Trail. Can Grandma make it? Of course. She was brought up in the hills of Kentucky. But how long ago was that? She doesn't answer.

Granted, I do have a frail, "skin and bones" look, but I have strong muscles.

The three boys make the trip the long way — by climbing every visible cliff and rock pile. Natalie, though often active, stays close to Grandma; I do believe to offer moral support. Son, daughter-in-law and daughter walk behind me most of the time, consoling me at intervals by promising that if I collapse backward, they'll form a life support blanket to catch me, and announcing that not far ahead is another rest bench. I don't need the support blanket, but I surely do need the benches!

Some fellow travelers who are on the return trip look at me as if they're thinking, "Will she make it? I hope her heart is good."

It isn't her heart nor her respiratory system, but where are those leg muscles that back home climb stairs twenty-five times a day? From the upper thighs to the ankles right now they are strained to the breaking point. But I do believe the support group behind me are all breathing harder than I am. I won't stop. I may not walk tomorrow, but I'll go to the top today!

I'm so glad I didn't stop.

In front of us stands the tall, round, concrete tower, and hallelujah, we can approach the top by a circular ramp that is just a third as steep as the half-mile trail behind us!

On top, the mountains are layered, not around us but under us. Is that North Carolina? In the far distance, could it be Georgia? Surprisingly, the air up here is warm, the breeze that was chilly below is quiet now. The evergreens that break through low, frothy clouds are crystallized with lichen. All of us, even the youngest, move slowly and silently around the tower, each one, in his or her own way, marvelling at the beauty of the panorama.

I say to my son beside me, "When we see something like this, it's easy to believe there's a Power bigger than we are," and he nods in assent.

Reluctantly, we start back down the trail. Some in our group claim the descent is harder — not for me! I may look a bit frazzled, but I'm doing fine. I even do a favor for others. Some climbers puffing their way up glance at me with an expression that seems to say, "Mercy, if she made it, I know I can!"

Later in the day, we go our separate ways — daughter, her son and I headed for Alabama, my son and family going part way up the valley that night so they'll have time for some sightseeing on the way home tomorrow. There are hugs and "don't stay away too longs" that make me feel good.

All through Tennessee the full moon lights our way, then the Georgia moon hovers even closer. Beth and I, above the soft-playing, stereo music, talk about families, the same people we know, long ago days, dreams for the children, what it takes for a good marriage, her work with young people in the university veterinary school, and how, in planting season, she still misses her dad, and so do I.

The miles roll by — sparse traffic, moonlight on meadows, and a nine-year-old sound asleep on the back seat.

Beth tells me to put the seat back if I want to nap. The suggestion sounds inviting, especially since there are still many miles to go, but suddenly, I'm wide awake. Before us, straight ahead, is the incredible Atlanta skyline — tall, tapered, tower-lighted skyscrapers that certainly weren't there when I worked on Peachtree Street during the summer of 1943. I had seen Atlanta since then but not for a dazzling night view such as this. I am totally overwhelmed by the massiveness and yes, the grandeur, and shocked that we are slicing through the heart of the city more rapidly than we could by-pass it! However, it's not the manmade, steel structures that impress me most. It's the huge, full moon hanging so close, directly in front of us, seeming almost to touch the tower tops, upstaging them with little or no effort. Again, I hear the same voice I heard on the mountain observation tower; I feel the same Presence. The moon bathes the entire closed-in city — all the girders and beams — and says, "There's a Power bigger than you are." I am sure I hear it add, " ... and don't you forget it!"

Off the super highway, onto a secondary road, onto a country road, into a familiar driveway. It's an hour past midnight, but lights are still on.

Martha, the youngest grandchild, her dad, and Amy, the chestnut retriever, had fallen asleep on the living room floor waiting for us.

I'm home now — another home. There's one waiting for me to go back to, and there's a family up across the fields waiting also, but for now, this is home, and I am glad.

I lie here thinking how sad it is that some in this world have no home at all!

Altogether, I've been over thirty-six hours on the way from the tip of the Shenandoah Valley to the outskirts of Montgomery, Alabama. I could have flown down (alone) in less than two hours — but just think of all I would have missed.

The New Dimension

I'm at my daughter's house in Alabama. Supper will be waiting when they come home from the university campus. Barbecued pork chops are simmering in the oven, and I was ambitious enough to devil a dozen eggs. Beth and seven-year-old Martha will arrive on time, but Thomas and nine-year-old Jimmy will be late. Jimmy has basketball practice, and his dad is the team coach.

An ordinary family returning from work and school at the end of the day? Yes, ordinary in most respects, but there is one difference. Thomas, the husband and father, is black. Jimmy is dark like his father with soft, ebony curls and enormous brown eyes. Martha is lighter with tints of chestnut in her hair and huge, dreamy, brown eyes.

It would be impossible to even estimate the number of times during the fifteen-year marriage that I have been asked, "How do you feel about it?" The answer would have to be classified according to tense. "How did I feel about it when I learned they would marry, and how do I feel about it now?" In teaching English for twenty-five years, I frequently emphasized the distinction between present and past tense.

Thomas was Beth's pathology teacher in veterinary school, and I think I knew early that it was more than a teacher-pupil relationship.

I must be open and candid, for if I am not, what I'm writing will be shallow and pretentious. When I knew the relationship was serious, I nearly went to pieces. At the same time, four members of my immediate family were facing physical crises — an excuse for my reaction? I don't know. I was sure that my life could never be the same — that even with the strength I was drawing from Jim, my strong partner, my world was crumbling.

Try to believe me when I say in all sincerity I am basically not a prejudiced person; I have never been truly narrow, for I love people too much. I honestly think I rate above average in accepting others as they are. I do not hurt others easily. I have always wanted life pleasant for those around me. In fact, the intensity of that desire has sometimes been a problem; at times — even now — my sense of well-being can depend too much on whether or not those close to me are happy.

You might ask, "Why then, when you knew your daughter was involved with a black man, did you crumble?"

Looking back, I know there were three reasons.

First, I had suffered all my life from the "What will people think?" syndrome. I grew up with it. In my early years, too often that question was the governing force in our code of ethics. Our life style was carefully monitored by the fear (and yes, it was fear!) of what others thought and possibly would say. I matured in some of my thinking as I grew older, but I had never dispelled that cloud.

I was constantly in the public eye; I taught school, did public speaking as a hobby, was involved in community affairs. Nothing I had ever done personally had caused turbulence or made waves; nothing that had ever happened to me had made waves. But this — my daughter to marry a Black man!

Also, the "What will people think?" syndrome had produced a kind of unhealthy, toxic pride. Often, the pride that builds in those born and reared in the mountains can be a positive force, but some of the by-products can destroy. I knew the situation with Beth would be discussed over and over, and I simply could not bear the thought of people feeling sorry for Jim and me. I knew they would say, "Poor Jim and Dess," and they would be so well-meaning, but I could not face the pity!

Second, no mother ever wants derogatory comments made about her child. I was angry, worried — oh yes, but she was still my daughter — high on a pedestal in our community. She was high school valedictorian, she completed a B.S. degree plus a veterinary degree in six years rather than the usual eight, she had always been considered an example for other young people. I could not bear to think she would be maligned. I could hear people saying, "I cannot believe she would do such a thing!"

I still feel that the third reason for my tears and sleepless nights was legitimate. If they married (and I knew they would), what would their future be like? Would they be hurt, either purposely or accidentally, by society? And if there were children, where would their places be? Would they find an identity, ever know who they really were? Would they find a world that belonged to them?

Never will I forget the day the call came that they would marry. I lashed out angrily, I pleaded. It did not pacify me when Beth tearfully said, "But, Mom, you taught me equality!" When my son and his wife stated emphatically that they could not believe I could be so intolerant and irrational, when a dear friend told his wife he was surprised that Dess ("of all people!") was so terribly upset, it didn't matter. My feelings were too raw, too eaten up with concern — and yes, I know now, with anger! — my daughter who never even needed to be given a curfew in the growing up years, who always conformed, who took a long walk in the fields when she felt antagonistic toward someone — could this be possible?

Many of my prophetic fears did materialize. Those around me and away from me discussed the situation. One friend said she couldn't believe God would let it happen to good Christian people like Jim and me. A family friend commented that he had always thought Beth was so refined and cultured. An educator friend frankly admitted (and I admired his honesty), "Dess, I could never accept it." A teacher friend standing by, not noted for her diplomacy, but always respected for her insight, calmly asked him, "Would it be worth losing your child?"

In the meantime, Jim, a dairy farmer from a proud, long-standing family steeped in old traditions, sat in his black chair and worried about whether or not I could survive the pressure physically. He knew he could. He worried because I was the one who went outside, the one to face the public, and he knew I was the overly sensitive one. I realize now that, even though he was hurting, he had faith in Beth, and even in me, and besides, he had long before mastered the technique of live and let live.

They were married on her dad's birthday in the university town where they were both teaching. We weren't there. I put candles on her dad's birthday cake and wiped away the tears.

One week flowed into another. I've never been a secretive person. I talk; I confide easily. I'm a "people" person. I knew me well enough to know that discussing the marriage with others would help heal. Jim, Nick's family, other relatives and friends in no way pressured me, in no way attempted to force any of their opinions, either negative or positive, upon me. A competent professional did clarify one misconception. When

I told him I was suffering from depression because I cried so much, he informed me that I was angry, not depressed, and that I needed desperately to learn to vent my anger.

Interestingly, Beth must have known that all along. From the very beginning, she had insisted that I say what I felt and that I write exactly what was inside me. Phone conversations were often loud, sentences in letters were like whips, but something good came of it; never did we cease to communicate. We were too close for that to happen. Silence between us would have been the ultimate hurt.

Jim had stated in the beginning that those who were our friends would still be — they were, and even acquaintances were kind. The entire community reacted without malice. Sometimes the pity hurt, but malice would have hurt far more.

I guess I should have known the kind of person Thomas was in late November after they were married. I had met him before, but my defenses had built a wall too impenetrable for me to see inside him.

Christmas had always been a monumental holiday in our family. As December came close, Beth called with a surprising message. She told me, "Mom, we know you all might not be ready for both of us to come home for Christmas. Thomas thinks that since I have always been home for Christmas, I should come anyway."

That night Jim and I did some deep soul searching. How could we even pretend to be Christians and let her come alone? I suddenly remembered the friend who wondered why God would allow this to happen to Christian people like Jim and me, and I remembered, too, that when I repeated the statement to another friend, she had said, "Maybe that's why it *did* happen to you!"

I recalled the family friend who said (and he meant no harm) he had thought Beth was refined and cultured. Thomas with a doctorate in pathology from Duke University, whose father had been a medical illustrator, whose brother is an internist in a Birmingham hospital, Thomas who gave time and money to help young people — not cultured? Not refined?

I remembered the friend who had rhetorically asked was anything worth losing a child, and I realized that Thomas had no intention of taking our child. He would allow us to keep her, even if it meant excluding him.

Next morning I wrote a letter to both of them, asking that they come for Christmas!

They arrived on Christmas Eve, not long after dark. We had, for the first time, lighted the entire downstairs of the old house with candles.

The tree stood twelve feet tall in the same corner of the living room where it had always stood. Strange — their trip was eight-hundred-miles long, and I had no way of closely calculating their arrival time. Somehow I must have known; not more than fifteen minutes after the last candle was lit, leaving the walls of the old house warm with soft shadows, they came. In the back of the station wagon was a beautiful console stereo, exactly what I had long wished for! Supper was ready to put on the table, but before we ate, we sat quietly in the candlelit dining room and listened to a choral version of "Silent Night" on the new stereo.

Something happened in the candle glow of that silent night. Call it Christmas, call it a lightening of the load of guilt, call it God — I don't know! I only know that for the first time in many months, I felt peace inside me.

Then I began to learn about my son-in-law. The stereo was no bribe. Neither was the miniature tea set from Switzerland, nor the music box from Cincinnati that plays my childhood-memory hymn "Amazing Grace", nor the crystal turtle from Italy, nor the ten-day trip to Nova Scotia and Canada in the fall after Jim left us, nor the trip to the west coast at Easter time (because I had never seen the Pacific). He gave without fanfare, not merely the material gifts, but a special, unostentatious brand of caring.

No one I ever knew (of any color) is easier to be with. In no time I realized that about him there is no showy facade; he is humble but not subservient, dignified but not arrogant, cognizant of the manner in which blacks have been stereotyped but not bitter. Our families and our friends have recognized in him the same qualities — and how could I have ever underestimated the substance of my community? There were no snide remarks, no hurtful words. When Beth was able to graduate from Cornell University with a doctorate in clinical pathology (primarily because Thomas assumed full care of the two children while she worked in the lab long into the night), my community said, "I know you and Jim are proud of her." We were.

One day last week I asked Beth what she considered the secret of their successful fifteen years of marriage, and her reply interested me. She told me, "We have made no attempt to change each other. We have never had a shouting match. If tensions rise, we each go off alone to think it through, then come back to talk it through." The formula must work, for I have not known a stronger partnership.

One factor is basic. I have learned that integrity is never limited to color. After rising high in industry over a ten-year period, making five times the salary I made teaching school, Thomas asked me during breakfast at my house one morning, "Odessa," — oddly enough, both my son and my son-in-law call me by my strange, first name — "would I be sacrificing my family if I took a cut in salary and went back into doing what I like to do?" Long before, our relationship had developed into an easy, same-channel exchange. I quickly replied, "You'd be sacrificing them if you didn't!"

So he went back to teaching, along with heading diagnostic services on the southern vet school campus. The opportunity proved timely. Beth, who enjoys both teaching and lab work, simultaneously received a combination offer.

I think often now of how much Thomas taught me. He (with my daughter's help) taught me that what lies outside a person means nothing, what lies inside is everything. The whole experience helped me become my own person — to be myself, stripped of layers of hypocrisy I didn't know were smothering me. I even managed to shed a great portion of the "What will people think?" layer. I know I reached a kind of self-actualization that left me not only caring deeply for my black son-in-law but liking myself better!

Do I worry about the future of the children? I'm not too naive to realize that the racial problem is far from solved, that prejudice and intolerance, even hatred, still abound. Somehow, I keep thinking that with the stability of their childhood, plus the educational, social and economic opportunities that can be theirs, they could, like their parents — by example — show the world the real meaning of equality.

Night before last Beth had a supper here for around forty graduates who had been in her elective classes. There were white students from Kentucky and Mississippi, black students from New Jersey and California, a lovely, brown-skinned lady from Trinidad, an out-going Chinese senior whose parents live in Hawaii — all coming together to share not only the food we had prepared, but hopefully, later, to nourish a sometimes sick society with strong principles and high ideals.

Last night the annual banquet for graduates was held. Each year at the banquet a noted pharmaceutical company presents an award to the outstanding teacher in each of the nation's twenty-one veterinary schools. Thomas won the award, and with it, a check for one thousand dollars. He plans to use the money to build a place for Jimmy and his school friends to play basketball.

I'm sure people will always ask concerning the interracial marriage, "How do you feel about it now?"

An early American poet wrote of the chambered nautilus that left one room and moved on to another — "a more stately mansion." I think I might have moved into another room.

I know that the experience added a whole new dimension to my world!

Saturday Morning with a Seven-year-old

She is still wearing her nightshirt, the pale pink one with two kittens, boasting black bows on their tails, etched across the front. Her hair, usually pony-tailed with a fashionable, bright-colored bow, hangs loose on her shoulders, and her feet are bare.

Most likely she still basks in a glow of self-satisfaction this morning because she made 110 percent on her semester science test yesterday; however, she missed twelve problems on her math test. When I questioned, "You missed twelve out of how many math problems?", her reply was quite evasive. In fact, I never did get an answer.

A large, wooden, double-drawer section from the underside of a recently discarded, leaky waterbed sits in the middle of the living room between the couch and the entertainment center. Her mother would be upset if she knew Miss Martha is lounging in one of the sections minus the drawer, and Colors, the brown, black and white cat — her markings are splashes, not spots — is drowsing in the section with the drawer intact. I realize there are splinters, and I realize her mother plans to convert the skeletal structure into closet storage space, but I do not reprimand. Any realistic mother should know that a built-in jungle gym in the middle of the living room floor would be too enticing for a curious, long-legged, seven-year-old to resist.

The dialogue begins. "Coherent" would not be the correct word to describe the content of the conversation.

"Grandma, which word do you like best — 'old' or 'elderly'?"

"Neither."

"But you have to like one of them."

I could not think of a defensive reply. She'd be confused if I told her I had never been overly fond of the "senior citizen" label either.

"Grandma, why can't you swim?"

"I'm afraid of water."

"You sure take a lot of baths. Why would anyone be afraid of water?"

"Because when I was just one year younger than you, I had to walk across a narrow plank ... "

"What's a plank?"

"It's a board. I had to walk across a narrow, board bridge. There had been a cloudburst ... "

"What's a cloudburst?"

"A really heavy rain. The creek water rose up almost to the bridge. I was half way across when all of a sudden, I got so dizzy I fell in."

She doesn't bother to ask how or if I got out. She asks instead,

"Was the water dirty?"

"Yes, muddy, too."

I don't add that back then, the mountain creeks served as automatic garbage disposals.

After I tell her, my voice pent with emotion, that luckily my dad was in the yard, heard my wild screams, plunged fully-clothed into raging, waist-deep torrents of water to save me, I expect her to be bowled over by the sheer dramatics of the episode. Instead, she calmly remarks,

"I didn't know there were creeks back then. I thought there were just oceans."

My head spins when I contemplate the aeons of time that have lapsed since nine-tenths of the earth's surface was covered with water. My ego is damaged, if not shattered.

We go from swimming to a related topic.

"What's your favorite sport, Grandma?"

"I like basketball."

"Were you good at any sports?"

"Not a single one."

I didn't dare venture off into hop-scotch or walking train track rails, for I figured the questions would be endless. Besides, I didn't excel in them either.

Her conclusion startles me.

"Then I guess your favorite sport is sitting down."

"No, I like to walk or move around. I never could stay still long at a time."

"All old people are supposed to sit a lot. The body breaks down before the brain."

I silently muse, "I hope so — I guess."

Being informed next that a certain kind of spiny-backed dinosaur had two brains — one was in his head and the other in his tail — is no consolation because she adds that the one in the tail didn't really work. She doesn't know why.

The memory of a seven-year-old is uncanny and dangerous. When grandmas have told them stories three or four years ago, and perhaps added a few colorful embellishments, they must be extremely cautious.

I now hear,

> "When your mother sat down on a water snake on a rock on the creek bank when she was a little girl and it bit her, did it make a place on her bottom?"

I hesitate. I had not asked my mother for that bit of information, but I'm quite sure that if I inadvertently change my tale from the original narrative of a few years ago, Miss Martha will know. So I come back with,

> "What do you think?"

> "I think it made a big place. Did doctors know how to put stitches in back then?"

One of her discussions proves to be both intriguing and educational. As she strokes Colors, the cat, still drowsing in the uncovered drawer, she asks,

> "Grandma, did you ever hear what one artist used for his paint brush? He was too poor to buy one. He cut hair out of his cat's tail and made a brush. People saw the bare spot and didn't know what caused it. It didn't

> hurt the cat, just made it look different. I'll bet Colors would look different, too if she had a spot cut out of her tail."

Do I detect a gleam in her eye that could foretell the sound of snipping scissors?

I doubt the veracity of the unusual trivia until she discloses the full name of the artist and adds that he later painted for the Court of England. I doubt no longer.

Colors is getting restless, so she ends the conversation with a final, significant question. Today, somehow, her prime-time topic is age.

> "Grandma, do many people seventy years old write books?"

The query reminded me of an incident that had occurred the day after I had arrived at her house for a visit.

Her dad walked into the room with a sheet of notebook paper and said,

"I want you to read something."

The teacher had asked the second graders to write what they wanted to be when they grew up. Miss Martha, in very legible cursive, had written:

When I grow up I want to be a writer
like my grandmother so I can write
stories that make people happy.

Later, I told her I wanted to frame the paragraph and asked her what color the border should be.

Her reply was immediate,

"Purple like my new hair bow."

Her bow is a deep, royal purple, and I'm glad, for believe me, that paper made me feel like a queen!

The Heritage

Household auction sales can be sad. I once saw an old lady with snow-white hair pulled into a bun at the back of her neck, sitting in a rocking chair on the front porch of her white, frame house, watching her possessions sold to the highest bidder. She said nothing, but there were tears in her eyes.

I've seen adult children whose parents were no longer able to care for themselves or their belongings look stricken when pieces of furniture they had grown up with went to the highest bidder.

It broke my heart when someone very close to me had to come inside and sit in her empty house while her daughter's toys were mulled over by strangers and later sold. The little girl, an only child, had died before she reached the age of five, and watching her doll bed sold was torturous.

Yes, auctions can be sad, but about them, also, can be an air of mystery and enchantment. A talented student of mine, Laura Miller Glenn, captured that aura in a eulogy she wrote to her retired auctioneer father. Her phrases pick up the enchantment — and the excitement:

> The morning glistening with diamond
> dew sparkles with first light's
> promise.
> Questions called in hushed tones

preserve the memories hiding in
corners of musty bookshelves.
Movements made with cat-like quiet
do not disturb the cobweb delicacy
of other's past.

The tables are set with Grandmother's
finest china,
dusty lawn furniture and
mysteriously
familiar steamer trunks line
the backyard with days gone by.

A hush filled with excitement
descends upon the rag-tag, royal
crowd.
All eyes follow the Stetson-crowned
king,
all await the piper's call to treasure.

The gavel sounds,
pronouncing the verdict to come
and gather yesterday.
The day begins
when the auctioneer sings.

Yes, auctions brim with sadness and mystery and excitement. I can remember going home feeling almost guilty because I now possessed someone else's treasure. Was I greedy? Pushy? Was I callous? Did I pay too little for a priceless piece of another's past? Then somehow, I began to question. Are auctions really sad, are they unfeeling? I'd like to know now that what I own would give pleasure to someone else.

A rectangular, gold-framed painting of a farm nestled in layers of Blue Ridge Mountains hangs over the mantel in my green bedroom. I paid five dollars for it at a sale — not much, I realize — but I'm convinced that the owner would be thrilled to know that every time I look at the painting, a feeling of peace steals over me.

And whoever owned the gorgeous rose-flowered washbowl and pitcher set — complete with smaller ice pitcher, shaving mug, toothbrush holder, plus the round, covered soap dish — would want me to see beauty in it. I did feel guilty many years ago when I paid only seven dollars for it, but when was price ever a measure of beauty?

I'm sure, too, that the owner of the dainty dressing table with three mirrors — the side ones pull inward — would be relieved to know that I bought it, had it refinished, and placed my favorite jewelry box on it.

Come to think of it, an auction of one's personal possessions could be referred to as a form of pleasure recycling.

My old house is filled with "things." Some are worthless, some are in poor taste and add nothing to the decor, but some are quite lovely. In fact, I consider all the gifts from family and friends lovely. When the time comes that I have to leave the old farmhouse — either to another residence, or permanently — I will go more easily if I know that later, someone will touch one of my possessions tenderly and say, "I like this."

Certain items I know my family will want to keep, for they know already that heritage must always matter:

> I'm sure our son Nick will want the walnut desk with the many pigeon holes. It was made before the Civil War, without a metal nail in it, and it belonged to his great-grandfather who bought the house he and his family live in now.
>
> I imagine Beth, my daughter, and Mimi, my daughter-in-law, will have to draw straws over the pink-upholstered, cherry loveseat in the downstairs hall and the burgundy velvet sofa in the "parlor." Both have admired both pieces, but the two girls are so compatible that, I'm sure, whoever chooses the short straw will not feel that she got the short end of the deal.
>
> Perhaps the first of the five grandchildren to become a parent will want the antique cradle. It could be said to have special meaning because I refinished it all by myself. The use

of the word "special" is questionable. After removing layers of dark green paint, I spread some kind of wood filler on it. Evidently, it was the wrong kind, for it turned the cradle a gaudy red; so I doused my cradle with a lye bath, eventually produced a passable finish, and never again attempted to redo a piece of furniture!

I'm sure one of the children will want to keep the two-tiered table my dad made during his lunch hours when he worked on the railroad fifty years ago.

There won't be a problem with Mother's quilts. She made two for me, and both are beautiful. Beth and Mimi would treasure either.

Probably, the one who later lives in the old house with the thirteen-foot dining room ceiling will have to keep the handmade, cherry corner cupboard. It's too tall to fit in the corner of an ordinary house.

I'm sorry about the oak rocking chair. It's most likely the oldest piece of furniture in the house, beautifully carved, and so comfortable! — so comfortable, in fact, that I am rapidly wearing it out beyond repair.

Does all this bother me? Not at all. I'd like for my two children and their families to take what they can use, or just want, or just can't quite see go to strangers (they can, with my blessings, give to my wonderful friends), but I do not want them to feel sad if the time comes when leftovers must be sold.

However, I do have a few specific bequests.

In the book's first essay, "No Price Tag on Suncatchers," I expressed my admiration for suncatchers that hang in windows and pick-up the colors of the rainbow, especially my round, crystal one. I decided, though, not to purchase others because so many facets of my life serve as built-in suncatchers.

However, within a period of a few weeks after the essay appeared in a local newspaper, four friends gave me suncatchers — all of them lovely and very much appreciated. There was no price tag on them; friendship is free. Later — and I know my generous friends would not object — I would like for my five grandchildren to enjoy the rainbows created by those suncatchers:

> To Kevin, the oldest, I would give the diamond-shaped suncatcher hanging in the kitchen window. Inside it are sprays of dried russet and gold grain. It has been Kevin who made me closer to the land. I returned from a trip when he was

only ten, and before I could unpack my clothes, he drove me out into the field in the battered, gray station wagon to show me how much the alfalfa had grown since I left.

I have two round crystal suncatchers with geometric designs that spray rainbows all over.

To Natalie, I would give a crystal one to tell her how much our after-school talks have meant to me. They, many times, have highlighted my day like the colors of the spectrum. I'll give her the suncatcher in the window over my favorite writing nook in the southeast corner of the dining room — the room where we had our talks, and I think she will know that those talks made me feel younger and helped her grow up!

To Jimmy, I would give the heart-shaped suncatcher. With his gentleness and subtle humor came a close bond, the laughter like the red squares inside the heart, the frequent "I love you, Grandmas" on the phone like my favorite shade of blue bordering the heart.

Eric simply must have the butterfly on the front door panel

because he flits about, moves fast, because his dark eyes always sparkle, and because many times my day has been brightened when the back porch, screened door slammed and I heard, "Granny, I need something to drink."

Martha would want the other round, crystal suncatcher. I know she loves it because when she was only four, it disappeared from the window in the upstairs hall. She had climbed upon the table under it, taken it down from the window, and carried it in her hand to marvel at the rainbows. I didn't find it for weeks. Her wonderful spontaneity is much like the forever-moving rainbows reflected from the crystal ball.

An inexpensive suncatcher, I'll admit, isn't much of a heritage. Material things, we know, are not really important, but they can be symbols. The suncatchers can be thank-yous to my grandchildren for all the times they have taken me outside to feel warm sun on my shoulders and for all the times they have rushed inside and shouted, "Hurry, Grandma, there's a rainbow!"

After those close to me have chosen all they want to keep, I'd tell them to put the remainder on tables, porches, along the yard fence, and let the gavel sound. If they feel sad about seeing my "things" go, I would remind them that heritage applies not only to family or friends but to anyone who receives from another — and I would emphatically remind them of the wonderful heritage I have already enjoyed. My heritage has been a life brimming full, not only with material possessions, but with love and concern, and from so many!

Let the crowd await the "piper's call." They will not disturb the "cobweb delicacy" of my past.

All this I can sincerely say because I have already gathered the harvest of yesterday, and because all my life there have been so many suncatchers in my windows!

"Suncatchers in my Windows"